TASK

 **Self-Reliance**

 **Self-Awareness**

 **Self-Expression**

 **Self-Esteem**

 **Self-Direction**

 **Self-Soothing**

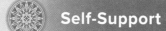 **Self-Support**

THE PRISM

THE
PRISM

SEVEN STEPS TO HEAL YOUR PAST
AND TRANSFORM YOUR FUTURE

Laura Day

*Spiegel
and Grau*

S&G

Spiegel & Grau, New York
www.spiegelandgrau.com

Interior design by Meighan Cavanaugh

Library of Congress Cataloging-in-Publication Data Available Upon Request

ISBN 978-1-954118-70-6 (hardcover)
ISBN 978-1-954118-83-6 (eBook)

Printed in the United States

First Edition

10 9 8 7 6 5 4 3 2 1

To the four corners of my reality:

My beloved husband, Stephen Schiff,

*My chosen brothers: my rock, Kevin Huvane,
and my life's exegete, Herschel Goldfield,*

*And, always and forever, my son and sun,
Samson Day.*

"The human psyche shows that each individual is an extension of all of existence."

—STANISLAV GROF

CONTENTS

Introduction

The book you have just opened, my seventh, has been more than ten years in the making. I have workshopped and tested it through countless sessions with thousands of my students. It is the next step in the Practical Intuition program, the next step in applying intuition to your life, your business, and your understanding of the world. The next step in creating effective change.

I call this study The Prism. It begins with an understanding of how intuition (mobile attention) and its active brother, healing (directed intention), can utilize what is commonly called "spirit" in a practical way, producing evidence-based results and affording you the opportunity to make a life-changing impact on the world around you.

There is a lot of mystification out there about spirit, about "oneness," about experiencing one's union with the Universal Mind, the Highest Good, Source, Atman—call it what you will. But spirit is simply energy. The human structure that creates what you experience as part of that energy is the ego.

The ego has been much maligned in spiritual practices. Yet it is the ego, and its adaptable yet precise structure, that allows us to channel spirit and create physical forms and events.

The rudiments of ego formation take place from the moment of our conception up until the age of six or seven, dictated by our genetics, our caretakers, and our caretakers' own lives and fortunes. That early ego structure then informs who we become, our vision, our choices, what we attract, our physical and psychosocial development, and how we experience our world. Distortions and limitations creep in long before we have the tools to understand them, disprove the fallacies, or do anything about them. Fortunately, we're not stuck with that situation. As adults, we can use intuition, healing, and awareness to restructure the ego.

When You Restructure the Ego, You Re-Create Your Life

Spiritual practices can result in experiences that are subjective and ephemeral. But the approach I outline in this book will guide you to a practice that is lasting, durable, and evidence based. You will decide on the results you want—and the achievement of those goals will provide evidence that this new approach is working. For many years, my online community has been using the tools I have developed through the Practical Intuition books and teachings, and the results have provided abundant and persuasive proof that humans can manifest opportunities in the outer world by restructuring their inner resources and then reconnecting to the world through these new structures.

In the pages that follow, you will find exercises that will further your understanding and spur your progress. Try them. Make them your own. This is not just a book to read and absorb; it is a book to *do*. I want my readers to use it day by day, hands-on, just as I do, just as my students do. In time you will find your life and your being transformed, seemingly without effort. Take this book as a user's manual for the human being, an active journey through self that demonstrates your remarkable ability to repair the damage done in your own creation, and in so doing manifest a reality of your own design.

It is your job to create your world.

Practical Intuition

For those of you who are not familiar with the concept of Practical Intuition—the system I introduced in my first book in 1996—a word of explanation, as intuition plays a role in the work ahead:

You may not know it, but you have the innate ability to get the information you need about anyone and anything at any point in time. That ability is what we call *intuition, extrasensory perception,* or, more accurately, *nonlocal perception.*

Practical Intuition is the approach I developed over a lifetime of testing, teaching, and practice that gives you access to these abilities, abilities you may not realize you have because they are usually not visible in your daily decision-making. Practical Intuition develops your capacity to predict what is to come rather than doing what we usually do: reliving the past and projecting it onto the present. It allows you to choose the future you want instead of merely succumbing to the forces that have always determined it. You become an active participant in creating your own tomorrow.

The information you receive through intuition can at first be confusing, because it comes to you through the same channels as your memories, your immediate environment, your thoughts, and the multitude of tasks and questions that are present in every moment of your life.

However, once you have a clear target or question, intuition will use anything and everything to get you the information you need. It will even use things you hadn't previously noticed—a picture, a book title, your ability to experience what is not in your immediate environment but is in your mind's eye. It will use memory, physical sensation, out-of-the-blue songs or storylines that feel like fantasy but end up verifying themselves over time—anything to steer you in the right direction.

Throughout this book you will discover spaces where I encourage you to tap into your intuition to find the right direction. As you become aware of your own challenges, intuition will provide you with solutions seemingly out of the blue—especially when you are doing the work in the Ego Center chapters.

At first, both the experiences and your responses may seem random and without sense. However, you may find that they prove profoundly useful as you learn to master your own energetic structure. Nothing is random. Everything is synchronistic and provides information and experiences that can be used to make seemingly miraculous changes. Even if you don't know which switch you flipped or exactly when you flipped it, you will see that life is *causal*. You make things happen. Using this book, you will learn how to manage that causality to create your reality.

You Already Know Everything

Intellectual understanding is overrated. You are conditioned to use intellect as your guide to the material world, but when you rely on it too much, you will spend a lot of time struggling with concepts that have no effective application in your life. Fortunately, intuition allows the intellect to expand in ways that create real change. It is our means of accessing information not only in the material world but also in realities that we aren't typically conscious of.

You can use your intuition to access parallel dimensions, the future, and even new perspectives on the past—all so that you can work with the dynamics of the moment to create a transformed tomorrow. When you do, you realize why, despite your best efforts, dreams didn't materialize, relationships failed, health became compromised, and your daily experience was more burdensome than you expected. You learn how to make simple, organic changes that will bring dramatic, desired transformation to your life.

If You Know How the World Works, You Know How to Work the World

This is what you will be mastering in the chapters to come. Mastery doesn't mean you will never have another loss or difficulty. Life is far too complex for that, and your subconscious patterning has so many layers. It does mean that you will experience your disappointments as guides to what you truly want to create, and you will use them to do just that: create your best reality.

Viewed from the outside, some of the experiences you'll read about in this book—and that you may have had yourself—may seem miraculous or even supernatural. Scientists can now directly observe how the brain responds to a thought sent from a stranger at a distance or to an image that a computer has not yet randomly generated.

Even in the face of such evidence, however, many skeptics will be convinced only by a direct experience of the phenomena I am talking about—or not at all. But belief isn't necessary to activate the tools of change. I have a favorite saying that I've been known to quote (perhaps a few times too many): "The good scientist suspends disbelief and runs the experiment anyway." None of what you'll read here requires your belief, but it does require your engagement.

As you work with this book, you will learn how to apply intuitive concepts in your daily life. I ask that you do more than just read or think about these concepts. You are your own best teacher. You are your own master guide. So, yes, engage. Try these ideas on. Practice them. Feel, see, hear, taste, smell, *live* them. Be open to a reality that encompasses them. Experiencing them will present you with a new paradigm and open up for you a dramatically effective path of transformation.

I suggest that you keep a journal for this journey. Besides what you will learn from these chapters, your own intuition will be giving you keys to joy and success that are unique to your individual reality—ones I could not give you because only you have them. And although we *are* one, you will learn in the next chapter that each of us has a distinct and sacred destiny. We are one another's guides, and not one of us is replaceable or superfluous. Value your uniqueness. Your wisdom elevates us all.

Simply trying out the concepts I present will activate a process of change. The exercises I provide will make the process conscious and add power and precision to what you create. Your subconscious will take in what it needs to create that change, and, when you want to accelerate the results, you will find yourself going back to do an exercise again, with even more rigor.

In that spirit, I want to start you off with a powerful manifestation technique. It will engage your intuition, your subconscious, and your ability to change your connection to everything in your life—all in a single gesture.

A MANIFESTATION TECHNIQUE

1. Take a moment to be mindful. Mindfulness is not meditation. Mindfulness is simply being aware of how you are, where you are, and what is around you. Take this moment to fully inhabit yourself *in the now* by taking an inventory of what each of your five senses is experiencing and using your attention to limit yourself to that experience of you, *now*.

2. Designate one of your hands to represent you, now.

3. Designate the other hand to represent the you that exists when your life is how you want it to be.

4. Don't engage your imagination. Simply remind yourself that the hand that represents your future intention has all the information you need, whether you are conscious of it or not. Don't search. Don't force. Don't worry if what you are "feeling" isn't positive. Simply allow the energy of the goal to gather as energy in your hand, as your other hand anchors you in the now.

5. As that goal continues to become real and solid in that hand, shift your focus to your other hand. Allow your mindfulness— you, in this moment—to fill this second hand.

6. Now hold your hands, palms facing each other, about a hand-length apart. One hand is the point in space-time where you and your goal are one. The other hand represents you, now, at this point in space-time.

7. The space between your hands is the distance between you now and you when your goal has been achieved. That distance is filled with obstacles, people, situations, and other dynamics that stand between your goal and the present moment. You may feel an energy between the palms of your hands as these two forces interact and recognize each

other. Your intuition will be aware of the outer world; your subconscious will be aware of your inner world. Both will work together beneath your conscious awareness to chart the changes that need to be made.

8. Now slowly, slowly allow your palms to come together. You are allowing yourself and your goal to come closer together in this present moment. Feel free to pause or even increase the distance between your palms until you sense an ease in bringing your hands closer together. This exercise takes the time it takes. You are moving a lot of energy—in others, around you, and in yourself. Insights may appear. You may notice a shift. Emotions may arise. Your environment may change. The phone may ring, and it may be one of your obstacles or one of your helpers on the line. Try to keep going until both palms come together comfortably and your desired future merges with this moment. As this happens, you are negotiating events, relationships, connections, and your position in space-time.

9. As your palms near each other, prepare for the moment when they will meet. At that point, the energy may dissipate unless you get ready for the next step: uniting that energy with the central energy of the self and letting it circulate through the center of yourself, out into the world, and back into the self in a timeless continuum.

10. And now your palms come together. When they do, as you move the energy into and through yourself, you have brought you and your goal powerfully into this moment, this place in space-time.

11. Hold the hand of the person who brought you here: you. Take your own hand as you would the hand of your most treasured and reliable friend.

We often get stuck in the wanting, the hoping, the fearing instead of anchoring our energy in the *doing and being*. Do this exercise regularly and you will find that your present and your desired future will come together more quickly. What we often underestimate is how deeply we change in this process. Be curious about the new awareness and illuminating experiences that come your way as you integrate this process into your life. Give yourself the suggestion that every time your palms come together, whether it is intentional or not, you will be achieving this result, this healing, this unity of your present and your desired future.

You have just done your first healing!

As you begin the work of *The Prism*, you may be surprised at how your life and your relationships transform over the coming days and weeks—and how you transform with them.

How to Use This Book

When I was a young psychic and healer, I sometimes made fun of the granola-eating, ugly-shoe-wearing, crystal-loving, yoga-posing woo-woos who believed in the power of the chakras—the seven energy centers of the body. Yes, I, a twenty-year-old, knew so much more than they. I did my intuitive work with scientists, not mystics. I was oh so superior.

In the nearly half century since then, science—always my guide—has demonstrated that sound, scent, vibration, vocalization, posture, currents, and color can transform not only our physical bodies but also our choices, our genetic codes, even objective reality. And—*shocker!*—in all those categories, the transformations correspond to the chakras.

Now an entire industry of gizmos has sprung up to change your vibe, your neurology, your cardiac rhythm, your vagal response, all entailing some alteration of your energetic "current." Look online and you will find that virtually every neurologist with an Instagram account and an invention has already targeted you with ads for their latest device. I must personally own twenty of them.

The truth, however, is this: the best gizmo is you. You are a powerful, interconnected, life-changing, reality-shifting machine.

What was missing from the woo-woo approach was a way to transform this ancient understanding of the chakras into targeted actions and replicable, verifiable results. Because much of this knowledge has remained buried in the arcana of Hindu, Buddhist, and Kabbalistic spiritual traditions, it has not been effectively applied to our contemporary lives.

This book lays out the process of taking this timeless knowledge, now substantiated by science, and using it to change your body, your relationships, your fortune—your life. The most crucial and yet radical discovery I have made during the years I've spent working with the science of the chakras is that these energy centers in our organism—centers both of our physical bodies and of our energetic or spiritual bodies—make up an all-encompassing structure that we have long designated with a much-maligned name:

The ego.

The ego is a structure composed of seven centers of energy—I call them Ego Centers—that correspond to the chakras and are so numbered, one through seven. This book proposes that our work on transforming ourselves and our lives necessarily takes place through the ego in its seven aspects.

By understanding how to "work" these Ego Centers systematically, we become the masters of our beings, our spirits, our lives. That is the program I present in this book.

Our culture has trained us to think of *ego* as a dirty word, associated as it is with excessive self-interest. Many of us derive our understanding of the word from Freud, who conceived of the human psyche as being made up of three parts: the id (our unmitigated instincts), the ego (the socialized, "public-facing" part of our consciousness that curbs the impulses of the id), and the superego (our critical, moralizing faculty). But I hope to engage you in the experience of the word's true meaning.

The ego is to a human being what the conductor is to an orchestra. It is not pure instinct and impulse, nor is it the colorless, characterless energy that many call *spirit*. Ego is the part of you that structures energy into a useful and physical form. It is the difference between the orchestra squeaking and squawking as it tunes up and the orchestra playing a symphony. Without an ego, you would be a useless mass of impulse and spirit, neither of which is capable of intentional creation.

The Ego Is the Powerful Machinery Within Each of Us That Has the Power to Transform Energy

We know from modern physics that everything is energy (an idea also familiar to those who have studied various spiritual teachings). Your ego takes this energy and, like a prism, refracts it into something else: your reactions, your relationships, your habits, your patterns, your body, all your physical and mental systems. And when that energy passes through you and then out again, *transformed*, it becomes your life. In that way, your ego "creates" your world from the energy that enters and emanates from you.

The problem for us is that this process happens unconsciously, without our being aware enough to direct it and turn it toward our goals. You are not to blame for this. Who you are and the world you live in are based on how you were built during your early years, both genetically and in the patterning that formed in your Ego Centers. But who you become is up to you.

Who you become depends on how you work with the prism that is your ego. It depends on your learning to identify the places where the prism is damaged, distorting the energy it receives, and then healing those places—so that instead of misdirecting our efforts at creation, our prism refines the energy and directs it toward our well-being, what we wish for ourselves and for the world around us.

This book is a manual for repairing the prism so your Ego Centers flourish, harmonize, and perform their functions in a healthy, resilient way. It puts all the work I've done over forty years of teaching into one system, a system that has saved my life and continues to allow me to choose who I am and what surrounds me every day.

The last century has radically changed what we know about ourselves. We have access to information the world never had before: a new understanding of neuroplasticity (the brain's ability to change itself), behavioral psychology (how our actions affect our brains), and epigenetics (the rather recent discovery that cells can change gene expression). Thanks to twentieth-century instrumentation, we have reams of documentation that confirms that extrasensory perception allows us to perceive and react to things that are not in our immediate environment or haven't yet occurred. As University of Virginia psychiatrist Jim B. Tucker has said, "Quantum physics indicates that our physical world may grow out of our consciousness." When I speak of intuition, of the impact you have on the future, or on someone you haven't yet met, or in a location you have never been, what I'm talking about is not simply my assertion. It is an aspect of reality that we can now demonstrate scientifically.

This data shows us that we, as human beings and human machines, have operating programs that are infinitely capable of change. Even so, it is hard for us to change, because the same system that keeps us running also keeps us stuck.

Because you are a system, the smallest of changes will transform your reality comprehensively. That is why it is so important to make the right change. How do you know when it's right? Because you see your life itself changing as a result, in positive, objective ways. You *verify*. It's not about how you feel; it's about what actually happens. Your goals materialize. Your health and relationships improve. You decide your own fate and work toward it, instead of wondering if this or that will occur. It is normal to kick up some dust when making a change. Difficulty does not mean you're moving in the wrong direction; difficulty can further your path toward a desired change.

These pages will offer you tools: a new thought to try on, a new behavior to practice, a way to use your perceptions differently. In the beginning, I'll suggest that you try one of these tools and use it consistently for a day, while observing how your life changes. It may surprise you that a small change can alter your life in a big way. The best way to get your subconscious—your hidden operating system—to use this material is to offer it proof that it's working.

As you implement the practices and suggestions in this book, you'll find that you'll engage with the world differently. You will find yourself collaborating with people in unexpected ways. You will catch yourself noticing things for the first time. The tools I'll teach you in this book will bring you powerful, immediate results.

You don't have to believe in these tools. They don't even have to "feel right." The system in this book does not require your belief. It only requires your engagement. The act of *doing* transforms what you see, who you meet, how you respond, and how the world responds to you. Do the exercises in these pages before you try to understand them. Ultimately, the results will provide you with explanations in your own unique language as you re-create your life.

I'll show you that what surrounds you is generated by your prism, by how you are structured, and therefore by the energetic signal you are sending out.

As you work with your unique internal architecture—your prism—you will intuitively know what is right for you. You will learn through doing. Even if you skip the explanation and simply perform the recommended tasks, the system will explain itself to you through your experiences.

In the pages that follow, you will find a series of charts illustrating the Ego Centers and their locations. And later in the book, you'll find full chapters devoted to analyzing each Ego Center in great detail, examining how they function at various stages of life, allowing you to assess whether they are healthy or damaged. I'll explain their capabilities and their limitations. You'll learn which Ego Center corresponds to your particular situation and to fashion an approach that is suited to your needs. You will find exercises, suggestions, and ancillary tools to use with each Ego Center.

There are two ways to approach this book:

The first option is to read the book in order, going through each chapter methodically and debugging your entire life. In this way, you'll start with your foundation and work your way up through each Ego Center until you arrive at a new normal. This process will remake your operating structure. Every change becomes an opportunity for healing and greater achievement.

The other option is nonlinear. You will see in the following charts that every life challenge has a corresponding Ego Center. If the conditions related to the Ego Center resonate with you, then dive in and do the work of healing that Ego Center.

Though we may have passing problems in one area or another, in my experience there is usually one Ego Center that requires lifelong attention—what I refer to as a "functional vulnerability"—and a corresponding Ego Center that compensates for the deficiencies in the former. The other five Ego Centers settle into some kind of general balance because those other two carry most of the weight. This often expresses itself as gifts in one Ego Center, such as incredible creativity or beauty, and a void in another that prevents you from harvesting the first one's benefits. I'll help you identify your functional vulnerability—if you have one—in chapter 6.

If there is a clear correlation between your functional vulnerabilities and a particular Ego Center, you can go directly to the corresponding chapter and begin rebuilding your life there.

THREE COINS:
AN EXERCISE

I'd like to take your hand and lead you into this book the way I lead my students in our work together: with an exercise that will position you for the deep, transformational dive to come.

Before you do anything else, before you even turn the page, grab a notebook and write down three goals for your future. Number them. You may choose the wrong ones at first, but don't worry. You are learning a process that will inevitably be refined in time.

Do not continue reading this book until you have written down your goals. When you do so, you will be starting the work of engaging your intuition. A goal can be something immediate or long-term, material or spiritual, just something that has meaning for you—don't labor over it. Write what comes to mind first.

1. _____

2. _____

3. _____

Now gather three identical coins and with an indelible marker number the coins 1, 2, and 3—one number on each coin. Find a pouch or small box and put the coins in it. You will need them later in the book.

1

The Prism

Have you ever shone light through a prism? If you have, you know that a prism takes a unified light source and translates it into a spectrum of individual colors. That is what the ego does with spiritual energy. Your ego is the prism through which energy is channeled to create your reality. A prism's angles are precise. The spectrum is generated by the relationship of one facet to another. So it is with your seven Ego Centers—the facets of your prism—which need to not only be clear and precise but also work with one another to create a strong and harmonious you and a direct connection between what you intend to create and its creation in your world.

The Refinement of the Prism Is Your Life's Work

You know you are on the right path when you create what you want to create and adapt to each life event, even the unfortunate ones, in a way that strengthens your ability to feel joy and generate ever more desirable outcomes. If what you create and how you feel about your life are not what you hoped for, that is due to a distortion of energy as it passes through the prism of the ego.

Until you do the healing work needed to repair the prism, the same original injury that gave rise to the distortion may present problematic situations again and again in different forms. Situations that require healing can be painful, but they are not punishment for your defects. Healing is the drive to be the joyful, powerful, and resilient person you were meant to be. Experiences don't just happen to you; they are *created* by you, often unconsciously. You will know you are healing when each day your world becomes more of what you want it to be.

As you exercise your intuitive abilities in the work we are about to explore, you will be healing your energetic prism—your ego. Life will then heal around you. When you become conscious of a dynamic that has been ruling you, it becomes a tool. In this way, you will be making your challenges conscious and giving your subconscious permission to make hidden information visible. Notice what happens as you read this book—who gets in touch, what opportunities come along, how relationships shift, and how you feel as you move through the moments of your life.

Healing the Prism

Every child needs to be loved unconditionally—at least in the
beginning. Without the mirroring eyes of a nonjudgmental
parent or caretaker, a child has no way of knowing who he is.
Every one of us was a we before we became an I.

—JOHN BRADSHAW, *Homecoming*

If you are joyful, successful, and in good health, you have a very
healthy ego—or else you are living a charmed moment of your life!
Yet life is about growth, and there will always be challenges. When
life becomes more difficult than what you can cope with, it is a sign
that you are demanding a growth that you are resisting. On the
other side of that growth is a life better than you can imagine from
your current experience.

Change can be painful, so our usual response is to resist growth
instead of welcoming it. There are areas of your life where you grow
and change easily, adapting to new challenges and using them to
excel. But there are other areas that lay you low. What is responsible
for the difference? Two things: your subconscious patterns and the
health of whatever Ego Center the challenge engages. Perhaps past
experiences have limited you with outdated "truths" and made it
hard to see the opportunities presented. Perhaps you see the opportunities, but old patterns keep you stuck.

As you go through this book, you will investigate areas of dysfunction and vulnerability in your life and turn them into your greatest
strengths. In fact, you have already begun this important work simply by being more aware. You have already begun to refine the prism
through which the infinite energy available to you flows and creates.

That prism, the ego, comprises of seven Ego Centers that develop from the moment you incarnate as a physical being. The way you project the energy of spirit outward from your seven Ego Centers determines what is reflected back to you through your relationships, your wealth, your health, your creativity, your physical beauty, and your impact on the people around you. How you *absorb* those reflections determines how the outer world impacts *you*—your ability to recognize what is nutrient and what is toxic, which determines how you make choices. Your interaction with those projections is where the change occurs—not within the prism and not in your own isolated self-reflection. Everything you do and everything you are in the world depends on the ability of your Ego Centers to project and absorb appropriately. That is where our work lies.

In the chapters ahead, I will lead you through the Ego Centers, one by one, analyzing them in depth and guiding you toward an understanding of your own prism, your individual interior architecture. But before we dive into the Ego Centers in granular detail, we need to prepare, so that when you get to those chapters you feel well-equipped to put them to work. To that end, we'll begin with a sort of wide-angle shot, a discussion of energy from thirty thousand feet up, as it were. Then we'll move in on our target, the ego. Beyond that we'll explore the concept of time and how to work with it in a practical way. Then we'll do some final preparation for the work with the Ego Centers, after which you'll be ready for the deep dive into the Ego Centers themselves.

As you work with this book, you will learn how to apply intuitive and healing concepts in your daily life to create verifiable results. I ask that you do more than just read or think about these concepts. Try these ideas on. Be open to a reality that encompasses them. Experiencing them will present you with nothing less than a new paradigm.

2

A Little Bit About Me

Before we go any further, I'm going to take a short detour to tell you a story—the story of how I came to recognize and understand the abilities I have and, eventually, developed a systematic approach to teaching others how to foster their own intuition and transform their lives. In other words, this is the story of how I came to write this book.

I am eager to share this with you because many of you are carrying heavy histories. You may be exhausted, even hopeless. In *Welcome to Your Crisis* I wrote something I firmly believe: "Rock bottom is a good place to start." We spend most of our energy holding on to what is. When that is taken away, our hands are freed to create once we have the tools to do so. Like you, I carry the story and injuries of my parents and their parents as well as my own. I remind myself that without these injuries I would not be a teacher. Though sometimes it still sucks! But you've got to make the scars useful, or they grow so tight they squeeze the life right out of you.

Your stories change as you look at them from different angles. The important thing is to be the hero of your own story.

This is my story, the useful one, as I live it today.

Intuition saved my life.

I was born, the first of four children, to a warm, funny, engaging, violent, narcissistic father and a brilliant, artistic, magical, loving, manic-depressive mother. My father had loved my mother, the wealthy, wild princess of their Midwestern town, since they were babies. When she was twenty-seven, he took advantage of one of her manic episodes to elope with her, against her parents' wishes and all reason.

It didn't hurt that she was an indulged heiress, who would one day inherit a fortune, and that he was from a family that once had means but had never quite recovered from the Depression. At the time of their marriage, she came with a trust fund, a housekeeper who became our nanny, a nice apartment in the East Thirties in New York, and a set of generous but interfering parents who knew that the magic he so loved in her had a dark and death-seeking side.

To seal the deal, my father made sure to get her pregnant immediately, and I gestated for three months on a cocktail of their passion and her daily Thorazine. My mother, as the story was told to me, strongly considered abortion at the urging of her doctor father. My own doctor father—nothing Freudian there—convinced her otherwise. I was born ten months and one week from the day they eloped.

My first memories are peaceful ones. My head on my mother's warm chest. Her songs in the night as I was rocked to sleep. A stranger gently closing my eyes with her fingers while my parents were away. My father later refused to believe that I could retain any memory from when I was three months old—until I described the bassinet with its green mesh and the yellow hair of the babysitter who lived downstairs.

My first year was happy. My mother was well medicated by the newness of marriage, an adoring baby to occupy her mania, and plenty of help—principally my grandmother and the nanny—during those increasingly frequent periods when all she wanted to do was sleep. My father had now attained the power and position he wanted: a wife who manipulated her wealthy family, a good residency at a top New York hospital, and a precocious baby with which to indenture his bride to him. I am told that I was the easiest, happiest of infants. This may have been a blessing of genetics and was certainly a convenient part of their love story, but I suspect that even then I knew I had no choice.

My mother often said that she was proof that breastfeeding was not an efficient means of birth control. She went on to have three more babies in the following four years. When all was said and done, we were four children, born from March 1959 to July 1964. It quickly became apparent that our parents had nowhere to put us. When my brother, Alexander, was born in 1963, they moved from the Thirty-Third Street apartment that my mother had had since college to the more commodious Peter Cooper Village apartment complex on the east side of Manhattan. It was the home of young professionals and their families, just middle-class enough to rub my aristocratic maternal grandparents the wrong way, much to the delight of my father. When, with the birth of my youngest sister, the noise became too much for my mother, she attempted an overdose with pills, and we children were all moved into a second two-bedroom apartment next door to theirs, a mirror of the first that had become available just in time for the end of her first stay at Manhattan's Payne Whitney Psychiatric Clinic, asylum to the likes of Robert Lowell and Marilyn Monroe. Being the mother of but one child, I am surprised she was not admitted sooner.

From the time I was five years old, my parents lived in apartment 3B, and we kids lived in 3C. Our nanny, Carrie Blackwelder, who also had four generations to look after in her own Harlem home, was the only functional adult in our ménage. When she was not tending to my mother, whom she adored, she took care of us kids, made dinner, and did household chores in both apartments. Since my brother was wild from birth and my father unpleasant to those he deemed beneath him, a variety of other household helpers came and quickly went. Only Carrie could make my father behave. (She was less successful with my brother.)

At five, I could heat a bottle and change a cloth diaper, a preschool skill set not uncommon in certain communities but unheard of in ours. My baby sister became so accustomed to small punctures from the Duckie Diaper safety pins, which were anything but safe in my tiny hands, that she didn't even cry when I accidentally stuck her.

I don't remember being afraid. There was always help. Help inside my head, help in the room. Help from people who had been with me since before forever, who showed me how to do the things I had to do.

Many children have imaginary friends. Mine never went away. There was an extended world I lived in that was so well integrated into what others might consider normal perceptions that I didn't identify it as unusual. At night, I would talk to my mother in my mind even though she was in her bedroom in the other apartment, and she would continue the discussion seamlessly at the breakfast table the next day—assuming, that is, that it was a day she got out of bed. When I conversed with people in the everyday world, movies would play in my head that illustrated what they were trying to say, and those movies would contain additional details they had not mentioned out loud but later were confirmed.

Someone took over for me at night when I had to light the stove and warm the baby bottle in a pan of water, not too hot, and turn the gas off again. He wasn't in me or outside of me but rather was sharing me, taking over the tasks, orchestrating my movements, and then leading me back to my own bed—first reminding me to pee.

As the years passed, my mother became more depressed and my father grew angrier, and that is when my memories fade. My most consistent recollection from that time is of my vigilance in keeping my mother alive. Even though I never spoke of it aloud, I knew that she wanted to die as much as I knew that I needed her to live. Of all the children in my family, I think I am the only one who can remember my mother as functioning, happy, adventuresome, and attentive. With the birth of each child, she faded further and further into addiction and depression. I am not sure my three younger siblings ever experienced any life other than the violent, hungry chaos known to forgotten children. Bad things happened to them. Things that are not mine to tell. My brother reacted by acting them out on others, and my youngest sister dissociated in a way that made her appear invincibly happy, if you didn't notice the extreme quirks in her behavior. It seemed to me my middle sister embraced the role of victim, and I was embarrassed by how she appeared to be perpetually holding her hands out for help. More often than not they came back empty.

As for me, I crossed into the world of intuition, where I knew how things needed to be done. And I followed this knowing, visiting the material world only long enough to interact with it appropriately and then returning to this other realm.

In short, I was raised by people only I could see. People only I could see led me to safe places and safe people in the world. People only I could see led me to "normal." On the other hand, the same neurological anomaly that made me able to experience these realities also challenged me scholastically and made me vulnerable to being used by others when I wasn't "listening" to the guides in my private world.

As we got older, and our parents were increasingly too busy to notice that four children lived next door, we kids found adaptive ways to survive. There was often no food in the refrigerator or the cupboard. We would cruise down the hallways, divvying up the neighbors' apartments and then dropping by to say hello, hoping for dinner. We were entertaining-enough company. Everyone in my family was brilliant. We knew because my father had our IQs measured and weaponized, and the numbers were loudly reviewed for us at every opportunity. I was at the bottom, and my sister who was next in the birth order was at the top. Nevertheless, when I was eleven, my father had me sign a document promising that I would not lose my virginity until I was thirty years old or had won a Nobel Prize, attaching the generous proviso that I would be released from this stricture at the earlier of the two events.

Whenever she was out of bed, our mother brought magic into our lives, especially during her manic periods, when she would transform our home into a Japanese teahouse or decide the Museum of Natural History could provide a better education than whatever school we were attending at the moment. At times you had to remind her that when she went outside, clothing was required. At other times, she would shop in a happy frenzy, buying Pappagallo and Marimekko dresses in every color if she found a style she liked. The rest of the time she was either locked in her room in a drug-induced sleep or fighting with my father, who was all too ready to unload his rage at her failings.

After an especially brutal fight, she instructed me to call the police. I did, he was escorted out, and one of them filed for divorce.

Soon afterward, on their anniversary, June 13 (which had fallen on a Friday the year they married), she attempted suicide again at a

moment when all my siblings were at summer camp—I never went—
and I was alone with my grandmother in the next-door apartment.

I had been asleep. Telepathy already active, I awakened suddenly
knowing that my mother was dying on the other side of the apartment wall. My grandmother didn't want to call the police. "The
neighbors will know our business," she said. "They have known for
a long time," I replied. It was a thing I somehow already understood
but had never spoken aloud. I dialed 911.

After the EMTs took her out on a stretcher, resuscitating her
as they ran, I found myself locked out of the children's apartment.
I no longer recall where my grandmother had gone—maybe she
was in the ambulance with my mother, maybe she withdrew as she
often did, not wanting to be associated with scandal. I know only
that, once again, I was being guided by people no one else could
see. I went into the adults' apartment, now deserted, and I searched
through my mother's clothes for something to change into. I wanted
her energy with me. On me. In her drawers, I found not only an
outfit but also a treasure trove of coins. Dressed in my mother's fin-
ery and carrying a bag full of change, I walked to Bellevue Hospital
to await her—not a great distance, which is fortunate, because, at
twelve, I had not yet mastered the First Avenue bus line. My father,
now separated from her, was not to be found. I never considered
trying to find him.

Not once, in the days that I was about to spend living in the
Bellevue emergency waiting room, did I think my mother would die.
I passed the time offering coffee and treats from the coin-operated
vending machines to the indigents there, who in turn cared for me.
As a rule, I was not allowed to drink Coca-Cola, but at Bellevue it
was all I drank. I don't recall sleeping. And I was in constant telepathic dialogue with my mother, pleading with her, breathing with
her, pulling her to me.

There is always a light if you look hard enough.

I have written before about the recollection I am about to relate to you, and every time I do, I beg my memory for a bit more detail, the better to thank the angel I already bless.

Before I describe this memory, I want to share my theory of angels. I assume it is very hard for a disincarnate being, energy without much mass, to move events and execute material functions. Based on hundreds of experiences recounted to me by readers and students, and a few of my own, it is my impression that the easiest way for a disincarnate being to get something done is to motivate an incarnate being to do it.

I believe that is what happened while I was living in that Bellevue waiting room in the summer of 1971.

After a while, someone noticed that a little girl was in the emergency room unattended, although in truth I had been very well and kindly attended by the people there, who, like me, had nowhere else to go. Each new shift supervisor, upon discovering me, would ask me who I was with, and I would always casually say, "My mother," without informing them that my mother was in intensive care and I had not seen her since she had been admitted.

Finally, one of them sent a chaplain.

In retrospect, he was very young and had probably not been in the chaplain business for long. He sat beside me and asked the same questions I had been asked before but with a gentle ease that was missing among the very harried desk staff. I ignored his questions and asked him mine, and, as he seemed to have time to stick around, I pressed him for more detail. "Why did they cut her throat?" "What is the whooshing sound?" "Why isn't she awake?" He asked me who had let me into intensive care so I would know to ask these things, and I told him no one had—I hadn't left the waiting room. He went to check the log and came back. I again demanded to see my mother, and he said that children were not allowed in intensive care. I insisted, and he took me to look through the little wired window in the ICU door, where, from a distance, I could see my tiny mother with my own eyes.

He sat on a bench as I walked back and forth outside that door for what I remember as a whole afternoon—but now, a half century later, who knows—and then he explained that he felt he had to get in touch with an adult of mine. "Her brain was without oxygen for a long time," he said, "and we can see from the machines they put on her that she won't awaken. And if she does the person she was will not be there." I told him he was wrong. She would awaken, and she would be just as she had been. I must have told him something more, because the hospital finally contacted my father, and my mother was then moved to the fancy hospital where he worked.

For years after that day, I would walk to Bellevue to see the chaplain, and, as he got to know me, he would ask me questions about how I could see and know what was beyond his understanding of what a human could perceive. I in turn asked him about the things twelve-year-olds want to know. He normalized for me a trauma response that could have resulted in my losing what little connection I had to my life and to ordinary reality. As I ate graham crackers and drank 7Up in his office, my intuition became one of the several unsensational subjects of our casual conversation. People ask me, "When did you first realize you had this ability?" I didn't. A young chaplain whose name I don't remember became the agent of my healing.

My mother awakened two weeks after she had been admitted. Her first words to me, after I put my hand over the gauze on her tracheotomy so she could make a sound when she spoke, were, "Why did you save me?" As an adult, I have so many answers that I wish I had given her, so many answers I have received from the healing work I have done on myself. In that moment, though, I was both crushed and silent.

My father was back in the picture by then, and I overheard him speaking on the phone about committing her to Payne Whitney Westchester. Like a good little spy, I told my grandparents. They flew into action, instructing her greedy brothers, my uncles, to come to New York and whisk her from her hospital bed, despite the tracheotomy wound still open in her neck, back to her childhood home in Shawnee Mission, Kansas. On the way to the house from the Kansas City airport, her brothers took her to a lawyer's office, and there, in whatever state of consciousness she was in, they had her sign a new will, robbing her children of an inheritance that none of us yet knew existed. (Many decades later, one of those brothers, having frittered away his portion of the fortune, blew his own brains out.)

A few months later, my mother showed up in New York to sweep us away to Kansas in pairs (the elder two first, the younger two second), but only long enough for us to spend a single semester at a Kansan school—in my case, Shawnee Mission Junior High. It was an attempt to use us as a "chit" in the divorce proceedings. When it became clear that we would be of no use, we were returned to New York and my father's care. But we were of no use to him either.

I think my mother loved us during her time on earth, but not enough to include us in her plans. Less than two years later, in her improbably grand childhood bedroom, full of faux Louis XV furniture, she finally lost her life to suicide. She was found half-under the bed, covered in her own vomit, having left a note on the outside of her bedroom door begging to be allowed to die. My uncle, whose job it was to check on her for the few days my grandparents were away, may have heeded the request, assuring his and his brother Fred's ownership of her share of a large trust. It was two days after my fourteenth birthday. My youngest sibling, Sarah, was nine. My grandfather, a prominent Shawnee Mission physician, made sure that the death certificate listed the cause of her demise as "heart failure." In a way, he wasn't wrong.

Years later, the principal of Stuyvesant High School, where my brother, Alexander, and I both went in the 1970s, stated that Alexander was the best math student in that school's hundred-year history—and Stuyvesant was the number-one school in the country for children gifted in math and science. Alexander later graduated from Harvard and obtained a master's degree in physics from Stanford and then another in business from the University of Virginia. He used all that knowledge to pursue many ventures during a colorful life. At fifty-one, he used that knowledge to print out an accurate map of the human brain and calculate the exact angle needed for a shotgun bullet's trajectory to kill someone without fail. He then put a shotgun in his mouth, positioned it at that angle, and pulled the trigger.

The apparent reasons were unconvincing. He had found out his girlfriend was cheating. The company of which he was the CEO had failed. My father, never interested in people when they were failing, had turned the flavor of his regard from pride to judgment. The truth was that too many narcissistic injuries in too short a time had battered a being who had been held together by pure will. The violence done to my brother throughout his life could fill another book. Suffice it to say that though he was handsome and brilliant and, for much of his life, successful, it simply wasn't enough. That shining structure had no foundation. He died in October 2013, two years and two months before the death of our baby sister, Sarah.

Sarah died by suicide on December 13, 2015. She was gifted in every way, and strong in the defense of those she loved. She was also stunningly beautiful. Her fat blond curls, long athletic body, warm seductive demeanor, and agile mind gave me my first taste of envy. I soon realized that it is better to take pleasure in admiring that which is not attainable than to resent or strive to become it. Sarah was my precious baby. At the age of fourteen, after being made unwelcome in her own home by our father after his remarriage, Sarah left, living with friends and eventually putting herself through Hunter College and then Columbia Law School. She passed the bar on her first try, after studying for it from a less stylish wing of Payne Whitney than my mother had inhabited. When she wasn't in Payne Whitney, she lived in Harlem and grew to love the children there so much that she founded a nonprofit, Neighborhood Kids of Harlem, to address their needs and heal their lives.

She couldn't heal her own. She was the youngest of my siblings, born into a heap of unraveled yarn that had long since given up any semblance of a pattern. As a little girl, Sarah, my sweet baby sister, didn't know how to ask for care, but even if she had, none would have been available. As an adult, she couldn't accept the love she received from her husband, her children, her friends, her brother-in-law, her brother, or me. She retreated and was, for ten years, a virtual shut-in. Gradually, she began to reenter the world. And there came a moment when she would either move forward or discover that she could not. She could not.

As I write this, I have just finished the obituary for my father, who died in September 2023. After divorcing my mother, he had fought her hard for ownership of his children and had won full custody. But when she died by suicide two years later, our value as battle pieces ended, and it became clear that the millions he had expected to manage by being our guardian had been appropriated by our uncles. Quickly, he lost interest in his admittedly difficult and traumatized kids. For my youngest siblings he had been pretty much the only parent. For my middle sister, born only fourteen months after me, he was the source of all power, for she was, when he liked any of us, his favorite.

My hatred of him during my mother's life—I was her champion— didn't leave me for many years after her death, but when I grew past his ability to do me harm, I realized that the battle I was fighting had been lost the moment she died. Hating him wasn't serving me. My recognition of that truth freed me to love him for what he was, and I took assiduous care of him during his last years, when everyone else had abandoned him. There was something immensely healing about giving him a few years during which he tasted the amazing life I had created for myself and those around me. Theater every week, dinners out, trips to London, a home that ran on a schedule with food in the refrigerator and laughter in every room. Intuition led me to a young carer named Mariam, whose father had abandoned her and who was willing to move in with mine. She adored him until his last breath. I don't think my father had ever before been adored.

Like most of my siblings (and the lion's share of all neglected children), I have been raped, molested, abandoned, beaten, hungry, shamed, criticized, and left alone. Nothing that happened to me in the outside world compared to the fear I felt in my childhood home. I didn't even realize that this level of terror wasn't normal until years after I left. The hyperintuitive alertness and openness that defines my career was the thing that helped me survive, and yet, once I made it out alive, that same state made every day unbearable. It didn't allow me to become a well-individuated, functional person. My template for life was very skewed. It has been my life's work to correct my course.

When I look back on those years, I realize that I was always aware of my connection to something greater than myself. I have always been both somewhat grandiose and scathingly self-critical, at once aware of both the potential and the reality of the moment. The gift of intuition gave me an awareness that there were tools I could access that would help me to survive and thrive.

It is my privilege to share these tools with you. It doesn't matter where you are now. High places make for big falls. The muck can yield treasures that, once you emerge from it, will give you a life only you could have and gifts only you can share with others. No muck, no lotus. I am continually a work in progress. My life is amazing and then, sometimes, I am blindsided by a piece of dysfunction that floors me. I use these tools, in this book, every day. Your pathology can be your potential when you are on a healing path. The world around you has a stunning way of being in resonance with your efforts and offering you its wealth to correspond with your awareness and efforts. It is alchemic and real.

Some of you had a good start in childhood and will do the work set out in this book to bring your lives to the next octave of pleasure and achievement. Some of you, though, like me, are survivors of life-altering trauma. A psychiatrist once said to me, "Survivors aren't pretty people." We don't have the luxury of being light and graceful. By the time we are young adults, we are often the hungry, PTSD-afflicted scavengers whose unpleasant traits kept us (and often those around us) alive when the odds were against us. It is challenging to unlearn the habits of embattled survival and to embrace the full joy and potential of our lives. It is not easy to abandon the defenses that kept us alive, even though they are limiting our success in the world and cutting us off from our being.

In all the years I have taught intuition and healing, I have observed that deep psychological injuries push us to either find the healing tools that later build our greatness or create patterns that destroy even the most amazing of life's offerings. Why do some of us survive and thrive while others, given similar circumstances, suffer and fail? How do we redefine the past in a way that allows us to choose how we move on from it instead of letting it dictate our future?

I sometimes think of this work as "The Book of Dead Siblings." It is an homage to their struggle. The same intuitive acuity and porosity that saved me was also alive in them, but in their case, it contributed to their instability. Genetically, we had very similar brains, but they lacked the tools to survive.

How did I develop those tools as I grew into adulthood? That's the next part of my story.

When I was in my early twenties, in the 1980s, I watched a documentary about ESP. Scientists in the film were describing extraordinary abilities that were part of my everyday life. I thought to myself, "Wait. Doesn't everyone experience this?" It was my first adult awareness that there was something about me that might be unusual—and interesting to others. It was an echo of the chaplain, a decade earlier, taking an interest in how my mind worked.

I can't lay out the timeline of what happened next. The intuitive part of me, which wanders around in time and space, obliterates the part of me that thinks sequentially. Instead of timelines, I remember scenes, snapshots.

I am in a large room. It is full of European and South American journalists, professors, and scientists who are listening to the results of tests that had been performed on me. One of the doctors participating in this study recounted this story in my first book, *Practical Intuition*. I was able to describe, to the group in attendance, the contents of a series of sealed boxes, without, of course, having any previous knowledge of what was inside them.

Around that time, I also remember delivering a lecture (with a Q and A) to an entire auditorium full of Italian academics—psychologists, neurologists, biologists, and so forth—about a series of experiments in which I had correctly met a succession of intuitive challenges. My clearest memory of that day is the feeling that they were assuming a level of sophistication in me that I didn't at all possess. I could answer any intuitive question they posed, but not a theoretical one. I remember, too, that they all seemed very old to my early-twentysomething eyes.

Later, I remember being given maps and being asked to mark on them where to find artifacts that were buried under the streets of Rome. This was, in fact, an illegal request, though I didn't know it at the time. In *Practical Intuition*, Dr. Bruno del Rosso related his impressions of one such event. Dr. Larry Waites also gave an account of some research he involved me in on new HIV drugs at a time when AIDS itself was a little-understood disease. I was so blessed by people like these who brought real-world under-standing to what is, in essence, a neurological malfunction. Again, angels.

Wanting to embrace these opportunities, but not all the madness that might come with them, I demanded and received a guarantee of anonymity if I were to continue working with scientific groups. Eventually, however, word got out, beyond the confines of academia. Suddenly I had a following for something I didn't even have a name for. I wasn't sure what to do with what people were now calling this "gift," so when they would ask, "Can you do ____ with this ability?" I would respond, "I don't know, but I'll try." And that is how, bit by bit, I developed my intuition and learned both its breadth and its limitations.

Years later, I was lucky enough to meet a group that was both conducting research and acting as research subjects at the Stanford Research Institute, Duke, and other noted universities. Most notable among these people was the talented artist and remote viewer Hella Hammid. Most of the test subjects would describe what they saw with words, making it susceptible to interpretation and harder to verify. Hella, however, was able to draw what she saw, and when the people she worked with uncovered a building, a burial site, an artifact, or, at one point, an entire buried city at a remote location that neither they nor Hella had ever seen before, it would turn out to be exactly like what she had drawn.

So now, instead of being an isolated research subject, I found myself in a group of colleagues, and I took great joy in the way we shared and developed our unique brains together, challenging one another to expand our understanding and the usefulness of our abilities. The late Dr. Candace Pert, the neuroscientist who discovered the existence of the opioid receptor, Dr. Charles Tart, and other remarkable minds gave real context to the wanderings of what would now be called our neurodivergent brains.

I was usually the youngest in these groups and, as such, I did not view this as "new" or "groundbreaking" research. I was surrounded by people who had already been performing these feats and studying these abilities while I was still in diapers. Some of them had esoteric inclinations; others were hard-core scientists who, in examining these capabilities in others, had recognized them in themselves. I remember a woman from the Basque Country who mixed intuition with her own cultural traditions and another who considered it a kind of magic, even though she also frequently harnessed it to work in very grounded ways with law enforcement investigators.

Coming from a family of scientists, I was interested only in the uses of ESP and intuition that could be verified. Although I experienced other esoteric phenomena, I needed constant reality testing in order to feel that I had not crossed over into crazy. I chose to work only with data I could prove, and since provable outcomes take place most immediately in the marketplaces we refer to as "business," I developed a reputation as a "business intuitive." For the last many decades, my day job has been to predict the future for large companies (without being given any information) in contexts that allow my predictions to be verified, and to teach others to use their intuition in data-oriented, evidence-based ways.

However, I didn't really put these abilities to work professionally until the early 1990s, when I found myself at home with a new baby and a need to support him. Again, intuition found me an angel.

In those days, every morning, I would talk on the phone for five or ten minutes with a currency trader whose wife was in my baby's play group. He would ask me questions about currency movements as I nursed my son, and I would tell him what I saw. It was in no way a romantic relationship, but my marriage was ending, and when I realized that I was in for an expensive divorce that I could not afford, I told the trader that I had to find a job, which meant we would no longer be able to speak each morning. He replied, "You make me money. I will hire you." And he did. Suddenly, I had health insurance, life insurance, and a paycheck, all for a few minutes of work each morning. I understood then that what I did could have real-world value.

In the years since, I have worked with CEOs, researchers, doctors, traders, and other licensed professionals as a radio tower for data. They work with me, I like to think, because I do not mystify what I do. It works, it is sometimes fallible, as are all things, and I don't cross professional boundaries. I am happy to obtain intuitive data on a patient for a doctor, but I do not make a practice of diagnosing for civilians. I will "look ahead" at the market for an investment firm but not for an individual. Intuition docs not supply wisdom. It simply gives information that can then be used to make winning moves and informed decisions. In the beginning, I didn't attach a philosophy to the process or even much understanding. Gradually, I realized that intuition is both an idiot's gift and the seed of every miracle. You give it a *conscious* question, goal, or challenge, and, with the right methodology, it more often than not gives you the specific information you need. If you are not aware that you have this ability, you are unlikely to use it consciously, although the subconscious has a field day using it to re-create habitual experiences. Once you recognize that when you need information, there is a part of your awareness that finds it, intuition becomes your constant guide.

That same capacity, which I sometimes describe as "mobile awareness"—the mind's ability to travel in time and space—proved to have another aspect, which some call "healing" but I call "focused intention." Before the COVID pandemic made in-person gatherings impossible, I would travel the US doing "laying on of hands" for up to eight hundred people a night, working alongside other healers whom I had trained in my simple methodology during a ten-minute presession—yes, *ten minutes!*—before the event. The dramatic changes—physical healing and also life fixes—that occurred in both the healers and the people who attended these events were inspiring. For me, the most inspiring thing of all was that these communities continued to heal and use intuition to guide one another long after our sessions: proof positive that this is a reliable process that can be easily replicated by anyone.

By now you may be wondering why I choose the word *intuitive* over *psychic*. In reality, that is what I am. I am psychic: I tell the future, I see the dead (though, OMG, it's so off-brand for me), I travel in time and space and describe remote locations, I can feel your thoughts and send you mine, but I don't want to be in the land of crazy ever again. I don't have a cat (well, not at the moment), I detest the color purple, and the only crystals I own have been given to me as gifts. I have an extra dose of an ability that is not *extra-sensory* perception—it is the way your senses actually work that you have been taught to ignore. So the word *psychic* makes me different and damaged. The phrase "practicing intuitive," to my mind, does not. I love doing events where in an hour I show you that you are every bit as weird as I am by having you exchange a quick intuitive (yes, psychic) reading for a complete stranger. Your psychic "hits" for you are not so impressive because you know you, but when you tell a complete stranger something about themselves that there is no way you could have known, it demonstrates, without a doubt, that you were as weird as I am all along.

And yet I still walk into the same walls disguised as opportunities, trip over the same old patterned reactions, attract the same devastating situations I grew up with, miss important cues, and plant little bombs in my own life. The difference now is that I often catch myself before the damage is done. The work in this book is lifesaving for me and it is never done.

Well, enough about me (almost). I have been telling you a bit of my story mainly to demonstrate one key point: *You don't choose the starting line. But you can choose the destination.*

As you now know, I did not start out in life in an ideal situation. In my family, staying alive always seemed optional. Uncle, gun. Brother, gun. Mother, overdose. Sister, overdose. My great-aunt Ruth, the family matriarch, went down in history as the first recorded intentional overdose of antidepressants. I was born with my limbs turned in, my spine in a gentle S. I have severe ADHD. People are often disappointed when they meet me at dinner parties. I am not wise. I am not even very educated or informed. I am intuitive, which has saved my life and given me the information, power, and mastery I needed to create the life I wanted.

Your pathology can become your potential. Mine has. I want to make you aware of this gift that is innate within you, to offer you the experience of forty years of teaching and over six decades of living, and to help you use that gift to change your life.

I want to be your angel.

3

Spirit

Three weeks before his death, Albert Einstein wrote the following about the passing of his friend Michele Besso:

> Now he has preceded me a little by parting from this strange world. To us believing physicists, the distinction between past, present, and future is only a stubbornly persistent illusion.

In October 2012, curled up on my couch in Rome, I began this book with these words. My then fiancé—now my husband—was editing the dialogue of a screenplay he had written about Einstein, and the quote struck me. But a few months later, feeling unready to write this book, I filed it away on my messy computer and moved on to another writing project.

Exactly a year later, in October 2013, I was in Arizona for the funeral of my brother, Alexander. My lovely sister-in-law had prepared a memorial card, and it bore those very words from Einstein. At the time, I couldn't remember how I knew the quote, though it resonated. I came home and began searching my computer for notes for a lecture, and there it was. I looked up, still not sure what I was seeing. My brother's memorial card was sitting in front of me, on my bedroom altar. I realized then that I had reached forward through time for that quote, a year before my brother died, and that this book, which I had then thought too risky to begin, was the book I now needed to write.

I have never taken so long to write a book. In truth, I wrote many books during those years, but though all of them were fun to get down on paper, none struck me as worthy of publication. Writing this one, however, remade me. The healing it created in my life has been stunning. It gave me a new understanding of the world as it revealed itself.

Before Einstein, science largely accepted the Newtonian conception of the universe's structure. Time was linear and marched forward, never backward. There were three dimensions, all spatial. But in the early twentieth century, Einstein's theories remapped the universe. Time was now understood as a fourth dimension, part of a space-time continuum. And with that shift has come a growing acceptance—at least among some physicists—that time might *not* be linear. That all events, past, present, and future, exist simultaneously. That there is only a constant *now*, a single point in space-time.

Energy and matter are a continuum as well; $E = mc^2$ describes their mathematical relationship. The universe appeared to be interconnected in ways that belied centuries of Western thought and even the evidence of our five senses.

When quantum physicists remapped the universe yet again, Einstein himself found what they were discovering difficult to accept:

that two subatomic particles across vast stretches of space-time could be intimately linked and communicate instantaneously with each other. They called this "quantum entanglement"—Einstein called it "spooky action at a distance"—a phenomenon that again seemed to contradict what our senses, and sensibilities, have always told us about the nature of things. Researchers don't yet know *how* this communication takes place, yet these discoveries of an interconnected reality have since been proven repeatedly and their importance elevated. The 2022 Nobel Prize in Physics, for example, went to three scientists for their research into "entangled photons."

What's more, a substantial body of scientific research spanning more than one hundred years has demonstrated that people can apply this interconnected plasticity of time and space directly to their lives. For example, dozens of research papers have been published discussing evidence that supports what has been called the "Maharishi Effect," in which groups of some size engaged in coordinated sessions of meditation and intention, have changed crime rates, raised the stock market, increased reports of life satisfaction, and reduced violence and fires in targeted locations. In the well-documented "double-slit experiment," a beam of light is aimed at two slits and refracted on the other side as a wave or a particle, depending on whether and how the event is being observed! In quantum mechanics, this phenomenon is known as the "observer effect," and it has led to a number of theories on how such an interaction is possible. "Remote viewing," a technique in which a subject can reportedly observe and accurately describe distant locations they have never seen, was used by the military during the Cold War to gain information on Russian activities. (The Russians were doing it too!) Even under laboratory conditions, people—you, we—*can change reality, predict the future, read one another's thoughts, and feel one another's feelings* with a consistency that goes far beyond probability. What were once "mystical" theories have now emerged as well-tested facts.

Thanks to the emergence of quantum physics, then, the worlds of science and spirituality—physics and metaphysics—now agree that you are part of an infinite, unified field of energy that transcends space and time. Quantum entanglement demonstrates that this field exists in a tangible, measurable way and that communication within this field is instantaneous, however improbable that may seem. How else to explain the remarkable data from an ongoing study (begun in 1998) in which the output and pattern of random number generators situated throughout the world were altered (in statistically significant ways) by major global events such as Princess Diana's death and 9/11? It appears that focused, intentional energy can take us deeper into that unified field, to a "place" where your ego and consciousness can more easily create the changes you want. And since energy and matter are equivalencies expressed in different mediums—$E = mc^2$—even the inanimate objects within your awareness are manifestations of that energy.

Everything, then, is energy. In other words, everything is spirit. The distinction between those two terms—*energy* and *spirit*—is merely semantic. I use them interchangeably. They represent the fundamental substance of life.

Which brings me to the concept that will run through all the work of this book:

The Concept: Everything Is You

We are not human beings having a spiritual experience.
We are spiritual beings having a human experience.

—Pierre Teilhard de Chardin

As the old Stylistics song put it, "You are everything, and everything is you." This is true because everything in the world—your lover or the lover you haven't yet met, your wealth or the wealth you haven't connected with yet, a chair, a train, a river, a rock, your neighbor, your jacket, your home—is an individuated manifestation of spirit, the single energy that works through countless fingers on a single, cosmic hand.

What you bring forth in your own life can only be created by the unique physical structure—the prism—that is you. But because you are not just an individual but also part of the unified energy of spirit, what you do changes us all. You are the co-architect of all reality. Every wish or challenge, no matter how seemingly superficial or profound—making more money, being the prettiest girl in the room, having the fastest car, dealing with pain, feeding the starving—is one you have taken on for all of us. What you experience changes everything. What I experience changes you.

In our human form, we experience ourselves as separate from the whole. We have the illusion of being incomplete and, at times, insignificant. That feeling is an outgrowth of our ego, our prism. But our separateness is an illusion, albeit a necessary one. In truth, you are never independent of the whole, and yet your job is to function as if you were so that you can evolve the whole. Evolve spirit. When you evolve, so does the oneness of which you are a part. When you navigate strong energies, such as rage and pain, or grow through courage or art, you teach us all to do the same. Spirit cannot do this itself without your human, material structure.

Because you came from spirit, you are surrounded by spirit, you *are* spirit, *there is no such thing as being not spiritual enough.* You don't need to make an effort to be spiritual. You are inherently an instrument for structuring spirit into matter. That is the function of what I call our human architecture, our prism. You can see the truth and power of this perception when you engage with it. You quickly realize that every person you walk past on the street, every utensil you use, every animal you encounter, every object you covet or reject, is an extension of you, while simultaneously working *with* you to create reality. Every moment is your opportunity to birth a miracle or correct a dynamic that has caused dysfunction. Events can't work *for* you; they can only work *with* you as you generate them. What you do, feel, experience, and confront—and how you change—counts. Persistent feelings of a broken heart, for example, can actually lead to cardiovascular problems. Likewise, buying your first car can translate into the emotional mobility that allows you to find a great job or relationship. When you choose, you change—and *everything* changes.

In this way, you are the warrior and teacher of spirit. And your journey, no matter how mundane and unimportant it may seem to you at times, is the sacred journey, without which none of us evolves.

When channeled through an individual, spirit becomes dynamic and transformative, and you, by being human, refine it with your imperfect courage. The question that should be constant in your being is not "Why is this happening?" but "What course am I taking, and what is the lesson I need to master in order to manifest what I want to create in the world?"

In that sense, our usual quest for transcendence and a higher meaning is regressive. When people talk about "becoming one with spirit," they envision a kind of perfection. But think for a moment about the idea of perfection—or, if you like, nirvana or true grace, whatever you may call it. It is static, even stagnant. You cannot improve on perfect. It goes nowhere, becomes nothing. It has no momentum or purpose. If the perfect being is omniscient, omnipresent, and omnipotent, it is also unchanging. *Unevolving.*

Now think for a moment about your life. You are born, you learn, you struggle, you love, you attach, you mourn, you reattach (despite knowing that every attachment brings with it loss), you create, you destroy, you mature into your full power only to age into dependence once again. It takes courage to live! Strength is required to go on each day in the face of our difficulties! You are often quick to condemn yourself for failings and weaknesses, but if you woke up today and met life in whatever imperfect way you did, you were doing the brave work of spirit. You are our hero. You are a superstar. Worship yourself. *And now do better!*

Now let's take this one step further. What goes for you also goes for the dynamics you are a part of. *Change you, change the dynamic. Change what is around you, change you.*

If your messy couch is you, do you clean it up to make space for clarity or for someone to come sit beside you and keep you company? Or does the messy couch reflect the wealth of your creativity? Do you appreciate it? Find its treasures? Only you know the answer.

A person who abandons you, harms you, or angers you isn't independent of you. That person is a distorted manifestation of disowned parts of you. So, given that awareness, how would you change in order to shift that dynamic? Would you use forgiveness? Distraction? Passion for your next adventure? Intentionally removing your gifts and needs from their life? If you take responsibility for what you wanted from them—support, affirmation, sex, a job—you put yourself back in charge of your life.

And if battles are happening outside you, they are also happening inside you. *Change you, change the dynamic.* If battles are happening around you, they are also happening within you. *Change what is around you, change you.* When you recognize yourself as the creator of your reality, you understand that you are also its agent of change.

When you understand spirit, you don't fear death. You treasure the opportunity and pleasures that being incarnated can offer while recognizing that *death is a homecoming.* In death, you again fully experience the unity of spirit, but you lose the power to change it. Life is the only place where the precious individual that you are can create, enjoy, and rejoice in the sensory beauty and power of physical reality.

You do have moments when you transcend your physical reality, and during those moments you may experience your pure spiritual energy—moments of ecstasy, moments of deep connection with another or a group, even moments when your physical functions pause, such as in near-death experiences. As Oliver Sacks and other researchers have noted, many people who suffer from a brain injury that results in the brain's losing its ability to limit perception report experiencing oneness with all time and all beings. Elisabeth Kübler-Ross, the psychiatrist who famously devoted her practice to the understanding of death and dying, documented thousands of near-death experiences in which perceptions expanded as the body ceased to function. For me, one of the most stunning confirmations was when Kübler-Ross did an emergency room shift on a national holiday. A family was in a car accident where some members of the family were killed. One of the children died but was resuscitated in the hospital. When he regained consciousness, *before* knowing that any of his family members had died, he reported that when he was dead, he had seen the family members who had died and not the ones who had survived. Psychotropic drugs, which alter the brain's ability to limit and discern, can produce a similar effect.

Most intuitives—and many physicists as well—see matter as energy that moves at a slower, heavier vibration. When you quicken and elevate that vibration through attention and intention, *this energy becomes mobile*, and you realize how porous and mutable material reality is. This is important, because if you don't know that something is subject to change, you are unlikely to try to change it.

So, "loosen" your "matter" *now*. Get up. Move around. Make a sound. Use your breath. Use that motion to loosen up the barriers you experience in relationship, opportunity, health, or any other area of your life where you want change and then *decide* what you want to experience next. Direct your energy toward what you want to create.

Why Intuition Works

The oneness of energy, time, and space that we've been discussing may be the reason that gifts such as intuition and healing work. You can predict the future because the future already exists. You can *change* the future because intuition gives you the opportunity to remake it in the present or the past. You can read someone's thoughts because the sense that you are separate from other people is not an aspect of reality; it's a construction of the human mind. Likewise, the sense that you are separated from the past and the future—from those who have died, those yet to be born, those far away—isn't the truth. Your deceased loved ones are right here with you. You feel separated from them because of the adaptive, limiting function of certain parts of your brain, parts that developed before you became aware of the possibilities of extended perception.

That limiting function *is* necessary, however. You *need* the pressurized experience of being finite, of being human. Pressure is what creates a diamond. Your job here is to use spirit to create in a material world and to constantly re-create *yourself*—to evolve spirit as you gain a mastery over your own life.

Apply these understandings for a single day and notice how your life changes.

If I Am One with Everything, Why Am I Brushing My Teeth Alone?

Almost everyone has had the experience of loneliness, along with the existential questions that often grow out of it. Why do I awaken each morning to perform such seemingly ephemeral tasks: wash, brush, eat, work, tend, and be tended to? Why do I love, opening my heart to loss? Why do I desire success, revenge, sex, laughter, connection—anything?! Why do I spend so much time and passion building what will one day be left behind?

In short, why am I here?

But perhaps a better question—since you *are* here—is this: "What do I have to master to be here successfully?" Followed by: "What are the tasks I am challenged with, and what are the enduring rewards I seek? What is the lesson plan?"

The objective of being human is not to *transcend* conflicts but to *metabolize* them. It's incumbent on you to develop unique skills to thrive and be part of a world you want to live in. And when you do, even when you feel alone doing it, your work empowers us all.

Matthew 18:20 says, "For where two or three are gathered in my name, there am I in the midst of them." In every religion, *connection* is fundamental to all blessing and, dare I say, all power. Connection creates access to the totality of energy we all share.

You are here to connect, to individuate, to teach, to learn.

To connect you must first experience your separateness.

When you are in a state of oneness, there is nothing to connect to. You are merged.

One.

You have no impact or leverage.

As you negotiate your way through the conflicts that arise between your individual needs and the needs of others, when you work with the ever-changing realities around you and struggle through them to build something better, you are doing what you were meant to do. *Everything you master is transmitted to the unified body of spirit.* That is why the work you do in this life can rightly be called a sacred task. Transcendence is a cop-out. We are not here to transcend our ego. *We are here to individuate from the whole and create material reality.*

Spirit can only evolve only through the efforts of a material being, and the human being is outfitted with a single structure capable of doing the job: the ego, our primary operating system. We will explore this further in the next chapter.

Before you begin the work of The Prism in earnest, I offer a couple doorways next that can amplify your connection to spirit more directly. The first exercise, Soft Focus, has to do with practicing subtle shifts in focus and attention, which will allow you to engage intuition and perception less limited by the blinders of expectation, experience, or even time and distance. In the exercise that follows, you will learn how to communicate with your Master Self.

Exercise

SOFT FOCUS

When you were a child, you developed boundaries around your attention so you wouldn't be distracted by multiple realities. As an adult, you have the capacity to consciously and responsibly shift between different states of awareness. When you change the boundaries of your attention, you open a portal for new perceptions and opportunities.

1. Randomly choose one of your coins and put it aside without looking at it.

2. Look at any point around you. Stay with the point you have chosen.

3. Notice your focus. You see the point and some of the space around it.

4. Concentrate fully on that point. Try to narrow your focus as much as possible. Notice what happens to your attention and how aware you are of your periphery. Your world contracts. Your field becomes smaller and more manageable.

5. Now allow your attention to go soft. Your attention is still on the point you have chosen, and though you are still aware of that point, notice how it expands and broadens until you are *also* more aware of its periphery.

6. Allow your attention to soften further. You will become aware of the room, people, scents, and sounds you hadn't seen or heard before. And if you allow your attention to soften even more, it will extend beyond the room to thoughts, places, ideas, the past, the future, other people. You don't have to direct your attention anywhere. In fact, it is better if your

attention hops around as it naturally does, and you simply notice where it takes you. You are *following* your attention, not directing it.

7. Now, if I were to ask you to notice where your attention started and where it went during this exercise, you might be surprised to discover that it has gone to information about the question or goal corresponding to the number written on your coin. Maybe it provided information—facts you can prove, predictions you can verify in the future. The experience itself will give you new and holistic insights into its significance.

8. Make a summation of what you perceived. Ask yourself, *If this information were a map with advice, where would it be directing me?* (It can also be helpful to share your perceptions with someone else, having their intuition interpret the information, without telling them about your goal or original intent. What they say may help guide you in a way you hadn't anticipated.)

9. Now look at the number written on the coin to see which goal you were doing an intuitive reading for. You may have discovered possibilities and perceptions that take you more quickly to reaching that goal.

10. Don't try to interpret your reading. Keep it, revisit it, allow it over time to reveal itself. If the reading was telling you a story, what is that story? Does it feel like it has significance in the present moment? The future? When? Be as precise as possible. Is there something from the past that needs to be addressed? The more you practice soft focus, the more it will enable you to effectively shift perspective, offering new avenues of awareness.

A note about such "blind" readings: Not knowing what you are getting information about helps to circumvent your habitual intellectual process, allowing intuition to be perceived. I know it feels strange at first to have the answer before the question, but it is one of the few ways to read yourself without your usual bias. I will be introducing processes to engage your intuition in problem-solving throughout the book.

Your Master Self:
A Meditation

In this meditation, you renew communication with the one who can best guide you: *you.*

You are an infinite array of lives and selves at an infinite number of points in time—all existing now, in this moment. As you live your life, you are evolving each one of these manifestations as they are evolving you. The highest, most evolved octave of each self is united in your Master Self. Your Master Self is the best of all of you at all points in space-time: past, present, and future. Your human struggles evolve your Master Self, but your Master Self can help you with them. You are your own personal guardian angel.

Now allow yourself to "perceive" your Master Self in front of you. There is no right way to do this, and in the beginning, as you get reacquainted with yourself, you may have to just assume its presence. Your perceptions will become clearer and more solid with practice.

When you were a baby, you were always in dialogue with your Master Self, but as the demands of being alive filled your consciousness, you may have lost the signal.

As you experience your Master Self in front of you, allow yourself to both speak and listen while you craft a working relationship together. What do you need your Master Self to resolve for you, guide you toward, heal for you, now? What does your Master Self need you to refine in yourself and in this life in order to strengthen your spirit? In order to evolve all spirit?

Allow this dialogue to open. Your Master Self is on your side. What you need, it needs. What you want, it wants. What you suffer, it suffers. Your Master Self can make sense of your struggles and give you the key to resolving them, and you will grow as a result of them.

As communication with your Master Self improves with time, create a simple signal to call your awareness to it. It can be something like putting your thumb and index finger together, touching your wedding band, thinking of a specific word, or seeing a color in your mind's eye. You can allow your Master Self to inhabit a talisman such as a stone, ring, or other meaningful object. Objects, rituals, and beliefs have only the power you give them.

Now assign your Master Self (or ask it to assign to you) a word or a cue, like opening a door or reaching for your phone or seeing the color red. Every time you do these things, you'll remember to be in touch with your Master Self.

In this way, you train yourself to be in instant communication with your Master Self and to use this connection when you need guidance. You can ask it to negotiate with someone else's Master Self and come to an agreement about some issue. There may be a time to speak to a past self or the past self of someone else. You can even work with your Master Self when you want to communicate with someone who has "crossed over."

Remember: a dialogue goes both ways. Speak, but remember to listen. Express your need, but be open to learning how to express it in a way that allows it to be met, which sometimes requires a willingness to accommodate a point of view you hadn't considered or weren't ready to accept. And don't forget that your Master Self's point of view is your own wisest council.

Draw, speak, sing, and/or write what you hear. Be open. Don't judge.

Your Master Self evolves as you do on your courageous journey through life.

When you wrote down your original three goals in the coin exercise, you gave your perceptions targets to work with and a structure to create from. That was the first step in bringing spiritual energy into the density of matter, thought into reality, and feeling into form. Through it all, you and the world around you remain energy, spirit.

Now rest in the following Healing Intermission as you integrate what you have achieved thus far.

HEALING
INTERMISSION

Randomly choose one of your coins and hold it in your hand or put it aside, without looking at it, until this exercise is completed.

As you read this page, take a long, deep breath, and, as you exhale, allow all your burdens, your needs, and your problems to release into the vast energy we all share. In this space of oneness, there is no time, no separation. You can heal the past, hold a loved one who has died or someone you desire whom you have yet to meet, visit a place you long for, heal the child you were, or create a future you desire.

All life—*all* your lives in their infinite variations—are happening now.

You are not alone. You are part of a unified field of energy. You are everything. Everything is you. In the brave awareness of you as *also* a separate and defined being, you are supported by this essential oneness. Make use of it, now.

Take a long, deep breath and allow life to happen in the most perfect way for you right now. Allow the energy of spirit to move through you and your life as it restores, guides, and heals.

Allow people and energy, your guides and your Master Self, loved ones who have died and loved ones who are far away, to join you now as you release your burdens and your dreams to this energy.

You may not find this a quiet or peaceful experience. New information, feelings, and thoughts may rush in. At the same time, you may also experience peace as you release your struggle—at least for a moment—to energies that are committed to your highest good.

When you are finished, record your answers to these questions:

1. As you experienced this Healing Intermission, what do you remember? Feel? Know? What was your hope? Who came to help? What did you release into the care of others?

2. Summarize what you perceived. As noted earlier, it is often helpful to ask someone else to interpret the information without telling them the intent behind it.

3. Now look at the number written on the coin. For which goal were you receiving intuitive guidance?

4

Ego

If you want to awaken all of humanity, then awaken
all of yourself. If you want to eliminate the suffering in
the world, then eliminate all that is dark and negative
in yourself. Truly, the greatest gift you have to give
is that of your own self-transformation.

—Lao-Tzu

A decade ago, I was at a spiritual conference in New York City. One of the speakers had to use the bathroom quickly before she went onstage. Three people were ahead of her in line, and she politely asked them if she could cut ahead of them so as not to delay her presentation. They graciously complied.

However, one of the organizers, someone who considered herself a spiritual teacher, sneered at her, saying, "Someone needs to check her ego." When no one responded to the nasty comment, she added, more loudly, "I have no ego."

I couldn't resist an opening like that, and I said, just as loudly, "If you truly have no ego, I have a good psychiatric referral for you."

You need an ego, and if you are old enough to read this book, you have one. The ego has gotten a bad rap, but it is the essential component of what makes you human and able to structure your energy—*all* energy—to create what you want in the world. Your ego, when it is healthy and functional, allows you to use information from both the spiritual and the physical world to make advantageous choices for yourself and moral choices concerning others.

Your ego grows and changes. Once childhood is over, you are tasked with mastering those changes. Ideally, that mastery increases as you mature. In fact, much of a successful adulthood is spent learning to heal and compensate for innate injuries to ego formation that occurred early in life.

When you heal your ego, you heal your life. That is why we are going to devote this chapter to understanding your ego and the following chapters to healing each Ego Center and its corresponding area in your life.

But before we continue, I'd like you to sit quietly for a moment and then write an adjective, scene, song, or phrase—*whatever* comes up for you—for each of the seven numbers below:

1. _____

2. _____

3. _____

4. _____

5. _____

6. _____

7. _____

Save your results, as we will be working with them in the chapters to come. When you have found your own way to do this exercise, you can see how I do it for myself on YouTube @lauradaycircle or on my website.

The Human Ego: A Job Description

HELP WANTED!

Candidate must regulate internal and external stimuli. Diplomacy required for dealing with the many parts of self and world. Must be able to navigate and assess a variety of ever-changing environmental circumstances. Must be able to set appropriate boundaries with others and self. Must be able to recover from continual injury and disappointment. Must be mobile enough to restructure constantly yet solid enough to maintain form. Discipline and regular management of the subconscious and the spiritual and intuitive world and their impact on the outer world are required. Good defense training and organization are a must. Must have integrity and excellent survival skills. Must play well with others. Must have the ability to compromise and to mediate wisely to arrive at the best outcomes.

The job is 24-7. Basic qualifications must be completed by age seven, and continuing education credits are mandatory and updated every moment. Compensation may at times be delayed, but the pay is good, including but not limited to housing, companionship, identity, worldly success, joy, health, and a supportive community.

Whether or not you want it, *the job is yours!*

The Facets of a Human Being

Your ego is your "I." Any sentence that begins with *I* is an expression of ego. *I love. I am. I want. I hate. I build. I think. I feel. I worship. I value. I defend. I sacrifice.* And so on.

The ego is the part of you that knows you exist. The ego is the part of you that can choose how you exist.

The ego is the prism where you structure energy into a useful and constructive form. Your ability to direct the energy of spirit to create a life that suits you depends on the degree to which your ego is intact and functional.

As a child, you don't have much control over how your ego develops. Your genetics largely rule your drives and impulses, and your early caretakers and environment affect other aspects of your inner architecture. Yet from a much earlier age than most people realize, you have the opportunity to alter that original structure by refining and redirecting spiritual energy. This is your (and your ego's) job on earth as an individuated, material being. But in order to do it well, you need to know where the kinks are.

We contain myriad systems. Most of them operate beneath our awareness. Nearly 90 percent of your motor actions, for example, are chosen more than seven seconds before your conscious mind becomes aware of them, while new evidence suggests that even choices beyond those simple motor actions are being made before we are aware of them. People who theorize about the power of attraction speak of changing your vibration to attract what you want. That would be a great methodology were it not for the fact that your "frequency" comes predominantly from your subconscious, built by your beliefs, experiences, and patterns. Your subconscious directs most of your life, even though it was assembled long before you reached adulthood or any kind of judicious awareness. Changing your frequency from one that creates suffering to one that attracts success and happiness is possible only when you heal the issues that created the frequency of suffering in the first place. Just as a fraction of a degree of change in the climate can cause dramatic natural disasters, minuscule changes in your life can affect it in cataclysmic—or miraculous—ways.

Earlier, I introduced the concept of The Prism—that your ego, like a prism, is the structure through which the spiritual energy of the universe is channeled, creating the spectrum that is your reality. By your reality I mean *everything* tangible—from your body to your home, relationships, experience, opportunities, illnesses, everyday miracles, anything that is material.

The prism's angled facets are your seven Ego Centers. Their structure arose when the sperm and the egg met and created the hardwiring of your physical being: your unique blueprint, your unique DNA. These Ego Centers have been impacted by all your early experiences as a sentient being—even those that began *before* your birth. As you developed further in utero, you responded to the physical and chemical blend within your mother's womb. At birth, your first experiences created a rudimentary understanding of the world and your place within it, giving you the initial framework that seeded your ego. Your caretakers' experience of themselves, as you perceived it, added to that framework while you developed as a conscious being.

Ego Development,
Damage, and Healing

Neurons that fire together wire together.

—Donald Hebb

Donald Hebb's famous postulate, later refined by neuropsychologists as "spike-timing-dependent plasticity" (STDP), gives us an accurate account of how your ego was formed from your early life experiences. See for yourself: As a child, were your needs, impulses, and actions met with satisfaction? Punishment? Indifference? Was your relationship with your caregivers pleasurable, painful, or altogether absent? Were their responses to your behavior consistent or inconsistent? Was your autonomy supported or thwarted? Were you welcome and secure or shunned and abandoned? Were your caretakers happy to care for and nourish you, or were they palpably overburdened because that nourishment and contact came at too high a price? How did they feel about their own lives, and how much of that feeling was absorbed by you?

Simultaneously, our early impulses and actions are met with a response from our environment, and that response further helps form our behavior and beliefs. It also forms our experience of ourselves. Your beliefs are not based on fact. They are based on your early experience, unmediated by a mature intellect.

At birth, you have three basic needs:

• physical protection

• nourishment

* human contact

and two basic fears:

* loud noises

* falling

How these needs were met and how these fears were managed form the first experience of who you are. If you habitually struggle with any area of your life or being, it means that somewhere in your development, your ego formation was distorted.

Perhaps you were made to feel "less than" or "other than" when your ego was growing its bones. Maybe you had to focus your attention on a parent or others in your environment to make sure they were safe, so you never learned to direct your attention to yourself. Perhaps nourishment was offered by toxic people or with burdensome attachments. Perhaps life disappointed you or pained you so much that you didn't develop the ability to deal with the foundational necessities of living and instead constructed fantasies that could not survive in the real world. Perhaps you felt so disempowered, or the influences around you were so destructive, that you gave up trying to create anything at all.

Conversely, you may have been loved and given all that you desired. You may never have cut your teeth on the early needs and frustrations that would have honed your senses of autonomy, cooperation, and competence. But this, too, is disempowering. Many of us, hoping to save our beloved children from pain and frustration, also save them from developing their power to determine their own reality.

Parenting is often a self-rehabilitative opportunity in which the caretakers reeducate themselves about what they missed growing up. For example, a child who never felt the unconditional love of her parents may eventually have children of her own and love them unconditionally, realizing only then that it was her parents' failing, and not her own, that made her feel unlovable. On the other hand, being a parent can often require the sacrifice of the parent's own ego needs, and that can also become dysfunctional. Children learn about the world not only by how they are treated but also *by absorbing their parents' feelings toward themselves and the world*. I have emphasized this because it's important to develop a sensor that can detect the worldview that became your own, not through direct experience but through osmosis—that very permeable boundary between caretaker and young child.

I am a very good example of this principle. I was surprised by who I became when I became a mother. I had grown up in a disorganized and chaotic atmosphere. But the moment my son was born, I realized I needed to structure and discipline my life in a way that I had never experienced, simply so he could be safe. That structure started with a tidy home, a regular schedule, a morning walk with my baby, writing time before he arose. Very quickly, this new structure organized my own talents in a way that proved useful in the world. By the time my son was four, I had written and published a *New York Times* bestseller and created an orderly and peaceful home in stark contrast to what I had experienced myself. Now, I am sure that I made many other mistakes that my son will correct with his children (while making his own set of mistakes in the process), but for me the magic was structure, and the desire to give that to my son created the life I have now.

Faulty parenting is not the only source of ego injury. Sometimes a child associates things that do not organically go together. If, as we learn to walk, our caretaker gets ill and is temporarily unavailable, we may conclude that autonomy equals abandonment. It may happen that just as we are learning to set boundaries with the word *no*, another baby is born, and we feel we have been replaced because of those healthy boundaries. I see many children who are given no limits and are allowed to run the show from an early age. These children never acquire tools, such as inhibition and self-soothing, that will allow them to manage disappointment and distress later in life. Their parents may love them, but the world will not.

What we call "evil" is the result of ego injuries that interfere with a person's connections to humanity and to spirit.

In 2011, a prominent neuroscientist, James Fallon, told the BBC that during his study of brain scans, he had come across one that clearly belonged to a psychopath—and had discovered it was his own! He had inherited a brain wired for psychopathy. Upon further investigation, he found that he was related to more than his fair share of notorious murderers. Yet he had built a solid family, won numerous awards, chaired the university faculty at UC Irvine and its medical school, led a rich, moral life, and harmed no one. His healthy ego, which he developed from an early age with the help of loving, supportive, and hands-on parents, gave him clear boundaries and redirected his genetic proclivities. The healthy development of his Ego Centers allowed him to have a satisfying and useful life.

We cannot lead successful lives, reach our goals, enjoy our lives, connect with satisfying relationships, or raise healthy children unless we understand how to use and heal our Ego Centers. Some people may already do so instinctively and unconsciously. For the rest of us, I hope these pages will serve as a workbook, a guide, and a tool for transformation.

5

Time and
How to Work with It

The Time Zones

As you reform each Ego Center, you will be engaging the four time zones: the past, the future, the nonlocal, and the present. Let's review them each now so that you can actively engage in a new way by considering the time zone to which you're responding.

The Past

We spend a lot of mental and emotional time in the past, where we have no impact. *The injury that you carry is rarely the original trauma itself; it is the pattern that continues in you.* You retraumatize yourself by re-creating the injury in many different guises. We often feel compelled to resolve trauma by revisiting the past, but that is a waste of time. The trauma isn't hiding from you. It is present here and now in what you can't accomplish, feel, let go of, or create. Reframing the past allows healing to happen in the present. A previous injury will be revisited only when its resolution is needed to accomplish your goals in the present. Adaptive repression has allowed you to function in your daily life and make the progress you've attained thus far. Your task is to consciously reframe the past to make it useful to you in the present and to harvest its gifts. Living this day well and finding every tool to help you do that will heal the past.

When you actively work on creating your life in the present, your interpretation of the past will naturally alter to address your current goals. Your past then supports your present and future life instead of encumbering them.

A word of caution: If you try to work on all your injuries at once, it will feel flooding, suffocating, and dispiriting. Work only with what helps you to function effectively now!

The Future

We also spend a lot of time in possible futures that are informed not by intuition but by ingrained patterns. Our "imaginary" future, then, is based in the past and not on intuitive vision. When intuition presents us with an actual future, it is for the purpose of enhancing our effectiveness in the present. When you spend too much time in the future, be it imaginary or intuitive, you neglect the opportunities in the present to do the very things that would create a better tomorrow. No amount of foresight can replace action. Foresight plus action, however, equals success. The future is yours to create, but only if your attention is in the present. As you work on directing your intuition more effectively, the future will reveal itself when it is useful for choosing the right path.

The Nonlocal

The evidence that human beings perceive nonlocally is now overwhelming. Telepathy (person-to-person communication over a distance), remote viewing (perceiving a location or situation at a distance), and other nonlocal skills have been thoroughly documented through research conducted by such major universities as Stanford and Duke. I referred to some of those studies earlier, and the results of many others are available for everyone's perusal, even on such straitlaced sites as PubMed (pubmed.com), which provides free access to a global database of scientific and biomedical studies.

What does that mean for you? Simply this: not only can you influence the world at a distance, but you yourself are constantly being influenced nonlocally. If you can send telepathy, you can also receive it. If you can view a remote location, as the participants at the Stanford Research Institute did while working with the CIA—you can also be viewed. "Distant healing," the idea that your thoughts and prayers can affect the health of an afflicted person far away, is another example of nonlocal influence that has been credibly documented. If an object can be influenced by thought, can you imagine how much you are influenced and influencing others in every moment? For these reasons, it is important to train your attention to function as a selectively permeable filter, taking in what is useful but keeping out what is toxic or disorienting so that you can act with integrity in your own best interests.

The Present

Throughout this book, I will ask you to follow your attention. When you do, you will be shocked at how little time you spend in the present moment. The mind is prone to wander, especially to past events and possible futures. Studies have shown that the majority of our thoughts are also negative or repetitive, circling around our regrets, hopes, and fears. Only when your attention is focused in the present, however, can you reconfigure your past, create your most desirable future, and use nonlocal information to your advantage. When you use the other time zones skillfully in the present, you are the master of your reality. In other words, your power lies in your ability to be mindful.

Mindfulness is often confused with a meditative state. In reality it is simply a state of being present in who you are and where you are in the current moment. Being mindful will change the possibilities you have in the present and future by keeping most of your attention and efforts in the here and now, where you can do things that make a difference. When you recharge the present moment by mastering your Ego Centers—challenges and all—you will find that you become the architect of your life.

Time Warps

Many of us get stuck in anxiety that is associated with times other than the present: the woulda-shoulda-coulda of the past, the fantasy or terror of the future, or fixations on what others are thinking and feeling. These are time warps, and they jeopardize your effectiveness.

Different parts of your ego structure may inhabit different time zones. Your heart, the Fourth Ego Center, may be too rooted in the past to create in the present. Your drive, your Third Ego Center, can be too rooted in the future to make realistic moves now. Your intellect and observation, your Sixth Ego Center, may be flying around nonlocally or be too porous to other's judgments or agendas, unable to respond to the opportunities and obstacles of the moment.

Information is available in all the time zones but is useful only when you harness it to create what is adaptive in the present. Maybe your Sixth Ego Center—observation, intellect, and intuition—needs to get unstuck by visiting the future a bit more. Perhaps your Second Ego Center—the framework of your creativity and nourishment—needs to visit the past to reopen sources of replenishment or to create some necessary boundaries. The more responsive you are to each time zone at each Ego Center, the more easily you will identify and manifest your goals.

But as useful as the information in each time zone can be, your power is always in the present. That is where most of your attention needs to be, and it's a demanding place to live! Mindfulness—being present in this moment and this place in space-time—requires us to be realistic, autonomous, and engaged.

You may want to be a writer/healer/actress/entrepreneur, and so you quit your job and put out your shingle, thinking this show of courage and faith is needed for success. The reality, however, is that refusing your obligation to deal with the present moment isn't courage; it's denial, and your subconscious won't support denial for long. You need to make a living and don't yet have the clients to pay the bills? Get a job. Make time for something new, but don't undermine your financial security.

We all want to grow but without illusion. Illusion gives us imaginary tools that don't work in the real world. Reality, when addressed, can be humbling, but it ultimately empowers you to see and enlist all your power and all the opportunity around you. Those people who address reality directly seem to instantly attract good luck, often in ways that are beyond what their old in-denial self could have imagined. If you commit to the present, *your* present, and do it fully, with no soft-landing half measures and no avoidance, you create an opening to experience immediate, dramatic miracles. This happened to me.

As I wrote my first book, I had a problem that wouldn't leave me alone. It had to do with my financial situation, which I couldn't ignore as I had in the past. The pressure of solving it knocked me out of my avoidance, out of my fantasy and my contained little world. It seemed unresolvable. I needed an unthinkable sum. I had to acknowledge the reality of my situation and my limitations and then organize my talents. Once I finally did, offers of help, requests for the talents I had long ignored, and other synchronistic situations put me at the center of a life that addressed the problem and bestowed on me so much more. I uncovered what was useful and powerful in me and my world. Not only did the financial problem resolve beyond my wildest hopes, but the change in me that allowed its resolution gave me the foundation for everything wonderful in my life right now, thirty years later.

One more thing . . .

Full disclosure: Miracles aren't all they are cracked up to be. Getting what you want demands quick adjustments, and your subconscious may object, invoking old patterns and memories and hijacking your intuition to warn you of the direst (if unlikely) possible future. Remember: *your subconscious is* sub-*conscious.* Each part of your awareness will band together *below* your consciousness to lure you into old, patterned architecture. Synchronicity will throw triggering events at you, and there will be sharp disagreements between the old you and the current you.

For years after my first book was published, I refused to hang out in bookstores, even though they had always been one of my favorite places. I felt threatened and exposed by seeing my face on the cover of my book, by being suddenly recognizable and on display. Strangers would walk up to me and say, "Tell me my name" or "Prove you're not a fraud." I had to deal with this aspect of myself in return for the ability to have a voice and pay the bills. But deal with it I did.

So stay on course with your goals. Let them be the lighthouse. The more doggedly you keep at it, the more easily you will accept change. When an obstacle arises, work with it as fuel toward your chosen goals. Address it, use it, get help with it—but don't let it stop you.

All Time Is Now:
An Active Meditation

As you read these words—*and throughout the next twenty-four hours*—experience all time as if it existed in this present moment. Your past, your past lives, your future, and all possible futures already exist right now, in this moment.

Allow what you are missing and whom you are missing to be a positive part of your experience *now*. Populate this moment in your life with everything and everyone you want. *Allow and notice instead of searching and imagining.* There are infinite possible variations. Allow the best future to come to you. I say "allow" because you can only create or imagine from what you know and from your perception of what you know. Your imagination has the blinders of your experience. You find what you are looking for, but you're only searching in the places you already know. Intuition and allowing open up new receptors for the possibilities that you may not know about.

Right now, allow access to all moments and possibility, all history, all futures, all of your infinite lives, relationships, achievements, and connections. They all exist now, each with its own awareness.

No time exists outside the now. Now is the dynamic space where you can negotiate everything. With this awareness, your goals—the very goals that you wrote down when you first started this book—will direct the future, and the past will rearrange itself to support your success in the present moment.

6

Tools to Prepare You for Working on the Ego Centers

This chapter is preparation for the chapters ahead that are devoted to healing the seven Ego Centers. I'll provide you with some essential tools that will be resources for you now, as you go through this process for the first time, and in the future, when you feel like you need a refresher.

The Components of Ego

The human Ego Centers, also known as *chakras*, are located at the major points of your endocrine system—the chemical messaging system of the body. The endocrine system is among the first bodily systems to develop in utero. Esoteric literature has long understood spiritual energy to be localized within the chakras, and each chakra, or Ego Center, helps to create your material reality from spirit. If your Ego Centers are healthy, this process will mean that spirit nourishes your life.

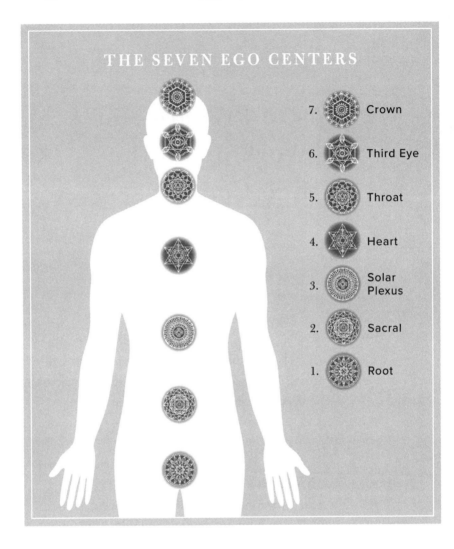

THE SEVEN EGO CENTERS

7. Crown

6. Third Eye

5. Throat

4. Heart

3. Solar Plexus

2. Sacral

1. Root

Your ego's well-being determines the three essential components of success: strength, flexibility, and resilience. As you do the exercises in the following chapters, look for these three qualities at each Ego Center and in your life as a whole. I'll be presenting tools and practices to enhance each of them.

Strength

Your capacity to affect the world around you is a function of the strength of your ego. Each Ego Center's strength lies in its ability to channel energy in the service of its task. You need to be as strong or stronger than the dynamics around you—the people, the events, even your old constructs of self—in order to prevail and create what you envision. Strength is an important component in resisting the conflicting events and forces that will naturally arise when you interact with your environment.

Flexibility

To respond to the ever-changing demands of our environment, the ego needs to be ready to alter its expression—for example, being accepting in one situation but aggressive in another. The same issue may require a different approach depending on the characters involved or your position in the hierarchy of the situation. Flexibility allows us to find what we need even when our external opportunities are not what we anticipated. Flexibility helps us to respond to setbacks, adapt in order to overcome obstacles, and locate the power and resources we need to respond to an ever-changing environment.

Resilience

We will always encounter situations where strength and flexibility are challenged so severely that they fail us, and in those cases we need to reorganize, reconstitute, and adapt in order to grow. These situations can come as gifts or as achievements, but just as an animal is most vulnerable when molting, so are we most vulnerable when preparing for a new set of demands. Resilience, the ability to bounce back when we are knocked off-center, is a vital ego quality for survival and success.

Your Ego Centers Are Your Community of Creation; They Build Your Life

Some of your Ego Centers will feel stronger than others. Some *seem* powerful but have a faulty foundation and let you down in hard times. Some of them are your foils—feelings, beliefs, and behaviors that always ruin a good thing. Some will thrive under various conditions. As you become familiar with your Ego Centers, you will begin to know which parts of yourself you can rely on.

At the beginning of chapter 4, I asked you to write an adjective, scene, song, or phrase for each number in a list of one through seven. The words you wrote corresponded to the feelings and experiences you had at each of the Ego Centers *at that moment*. If you do the same exercise again now, you might get very different responses. This is a good exercise to do at regular intervals to help you navigate your ego challenges. If you do it quickly, your conscious mind won't have time to filter out your more direct and instantaneous intuitive knowing. Keep your answers handy as you consider the qualities of each Ego Center.

Now look at those seven words, phrases, songs, or scenes you wrote down earlier. What do they say about how you experienced each Ego Center in that moment?

Next, you will find a numbered list of the Ego Centers and a description of some of their individual functions. As you read each one, notice how that Ego Center may have been strengthened or challenged not only by your own early experience but also by your caretakers' experiences of themselves and the world. Even if you don't have memories you trust, notice which feelings, scenes, and/or people come to your awareness as you read them.

The Ego Centers and Their Functions

1. **First Ego Center:** Your ability to be supported, grounded, safe, welcomed by the outside world, and to live in wealth and power. Your home in all its iterations.

2. **Second Ego Center:** Your ability to earn/create/attract sufficient resources to sustain yourself and feel as though you have enough. Your relationship to nourishment and pleasure. Your safe boundaries.

3. **Third Ego Center:** Your ability to manifest your desires, feel powerful, and have a clear direction in life. Your sense of purpose.

4. **Fourth Ego Center:** Your ability to feel loved and to find, develop, and maintain mutually loving relationships. Your ability to be valued and compensated for who you are and what you do.

5. **Fifth Ego Center:** Your ability to express yourself in a way that is authentic and compelling. The power and ability of your voice to impact others and the world around you.

6. **Sixth Ego Center:** Your ability to have clear, accurate, and actionable insights about yourself and the world around you. Your ability to plan ahead to meet your needs and avoid danger.

7. **Seventh Ego Center:** Your ability to access the energy necessary to create consistently in the world. Your right to your share of all the wonderful things, people, and experiences life has to offer. Connection. Your ability to manifest "miracles."

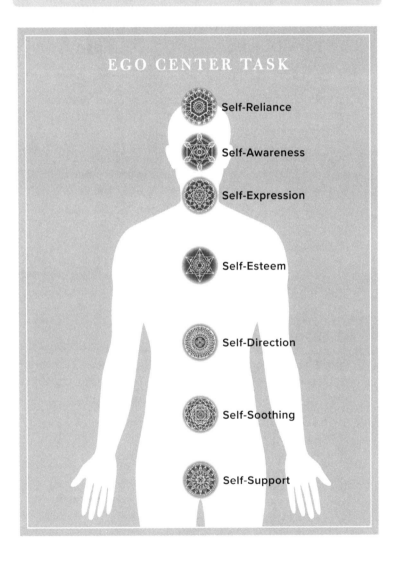

EGO CENTER TASK

Self-Reliance

Self-Awareness

Self-Expression

Self-Esteem

Self-Direction

Self-Soothing

Self-Support

If these structures began to develop in a healthy way in early childhood (the first six to seven years of life), you will be able to evolve them more easily in the adult world by having developed the following skills:

1. **Self-Support:** You find appropriate support in yourself and in the world.

2. **Self-Soothing:** You find appropriate nourishment in yourself and in the world.

3. **Self-Direction:** You direct yourself and others powerfully and appropriately in the world.

4. **Self-Love/Self-Esteem:** You have a sense of self-worth, are valued, and create value in the world.

5. **Self-Expression:** You communicate effectively, convincingly, and honestly, both to yourself and to others.

6. **Self-Awareness:** You accurately interpret and perceive the information you need about yourself and the world.

7. **Self-Reliance:** You know that you are everything and you can create anything through your individual efforts.

The following list contains seven conditions (one for each Ego Center) that are necessary for a healthy ego. To have a self-protective, loving ego as an adult, the rudiments of each statement must have been true by the time you reached the age of six or seven:

1. I am safe.

2. I am nourished.

3. I am guided.

4. I am valued.

5. I am heard.

6. I know.

7. I belong.

Reread the above list of conditions and notice how and when you may have received confusing messages about them in your childhood. Even if you don't remember everything directly, you can retroactively access the answers by recognizing the painful areas in your life today. If any statement on this list does not feel true to you, it represents a wound that needs to heal.

The Three Life Phases

The Ego Centers are developed through three life phases: birth (birth through infancy), development (toddlerhood through age six or seven), maturity (age six or seven into adulthood). It is critical that the ego develops through these phases in consecutive order, though the ego centers will mature concurrently. Any disruption of this process requires going back to the stage where development was arrested and healing it—revisiting that Ego Center's developmental stage, with yourself in the role of caretaker of the injured part of you. That is how you heal the prism that is your ego.

Below is a series of key words that can guide you through the Ego Centers' three phases.

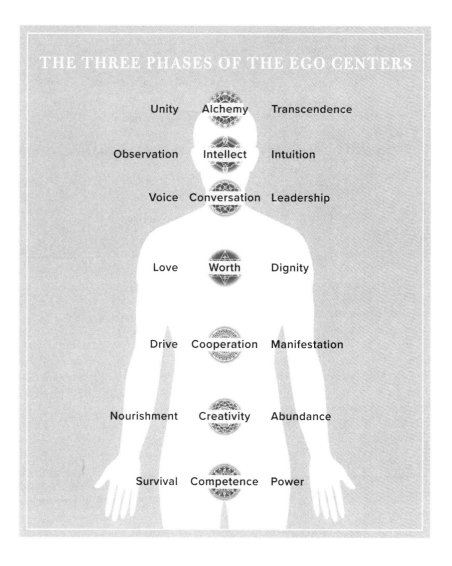

THE THREE PHASES OF THE EGO CENTERS

Unity	Alchemy	Transcendence
Observation	Intellect	Intuition
Voice	Conversation	Leadership
Love	Worth	Dignity
Drive	Cooperation	Manifestation
Nourishment	Creativity	Abundance
Survival	Competence	Power

Ego Center Key Words for the Life Phases
of Birth / Development / Maturity

First Ego Center	survival / competence / power
Second Ego Center	nourishment / creativity / abundance
Third Ego Center	drive / cooperation / manifestation
Fourth Ego Center	love / worth / dignity
Fifth Ego Center	voice / conversation / leadership
Sixth Ego Center	observation / intellect / intuition
Seventh Ego Center	unity / alchemy / transcendence

Every being has a birthright that correlates to the seven Ego Centers. That birthright, and how fully it is (or is not) experienced, sets the foundation for all further development. Let's take the Fourth Ego Center, your Heart Center, as an example.

At birth, your Heart Center is activated by being loved by your caretakers. Your worth is in your being. In other words, if your experience as a young child was healthy, you received unconditional love. You didn't have to be worthy. Your being was enough to give you value.

In development, as you interact with a larger world, you take that sense of worth that is now a part of you and it illuminates where you can add value to people and situations that are meaningful to you. Because you know the feeling of being valued and valuing others, you have a natural filter for devaluing situations and you avoid them.

In maturity, your value and beauty are a part of who you are. Your presence dignifies everything around you as you reflect—and bring out—the love and value in others. You live with an almost effortless grace.

However, if you were never afforded a sense of self-worth as a child, or if you had to demonstrate value or fill a role for your caretakers before you could passively absorb this birthright, there is healing to be done. You may enter into relationships in a variety of dysfunctional ways. You may, for example, use your Heart Center only to meet your survival needs and sacrifice the pleasure and strength that come from an honest, mutually supportive relationship. You may engage in relationships where you aren't properly valued in love, work, even parenting. If you were forced to be a caretaker too early, you may not know how to love yourself or identify others who can love you. The Ego Centers need to develop in *consecutive* steps, and precocious children who skip steps (often revered as "Indigo Children") are injured beings who create unsatisfying worlds to live in. Their abilities have no foundation and are not the gifts of maturity but the incomplete and unreliable tools of basic survival.

My own greatest injury was in the development of my Sixth Ego Center, whose first experience should be to observe the world and learn in safety, before having to assess and react. Only after that can the intellect develop in a functional way, and then intuition can be added to lend originality, suppleness, and breadth. But people like me, who apply intuition at too early an age, do so because of trauma, not because we're evolved. We responded to urgent situations that were way above our pay grade long before we acquired the intellectual skills to do so.

Many of the challenges in my own life arise because I still fail to see the obvious or think things through productively. On top of that, I have the additional neurological challenge of ADHD, which often prevents me from using my intellect effectively or from being centered enough to observe. My mind is often too anxiety-ridden to enjoy the amazing life that intuition has provided me with. I miss cues. I have allowed people and situations into my life that create crisis. On the other hand, my Sixth Ego Center's gift of intuition—overdeveloped because of that early damage—puts food

EGO MANIFESTATION IN THE WORLD

 7. Ease • Synchronicity • Power • Belonging • Faith • Resources • Ecstasy • Miracles

 6. Curiosity • Engagement • Effective Foresight • Persuasiveness • Vision • Good Luck

 5. Respect • Identity • Recognition • Choice • Truth • A Following • Agreement

 4. Connection • Love • Value • Purpose • Resilience • Mutuality • Enchantment • Beauty

 3. Options • Impact • Purpose • Flexibility • Cooperation • Manifestation • Vitality

 2. Wealth • Pleasure • Reproduction • Self-Regulation • Boundaries • Health • Attractiveness

 1. Safety • Belonging • Entitlement • Family • Presence • Structure • Power

on my table. I know that when my life goes haywire, I need to investigate the pattern of injury in that particular Ego Center and cultivate intellectual and rational understanding—or ask others who are more skilled in these things to assist me.

We all have Ego Centers that are unbalanced in some way. Being aware of your vulnerabilities can be a powerful tool for discovering your strengths and healing egoic injuries. Once healed, your injury can finally release your potential.

Goals and the Ego Centers

The Ego Centers dictate your ability to manifest what you want in the world—your goals. In the chapters to come we will be empowering that ability. But the first step is *awareness*. Your awareness of how the Ego Centers operate in you will allow your intellect and intuition to work together to heal your life.

The chart below lists the gifts that healthy Ego Centers attract to us from the world.

First Ego Center	safety / belonging / entitlement / family / presence / structure / power
Second Ego Center	wealth / pleasure / reproduction / self-regulation / boundaries / health / attractiveness
Third Ego Center	options / impact / purpose / flexibility / cooperation / manifestation / vitality
Fourth Ego Center	connection / love / value / purpose / resilience / mutuality / enchantment / beauty

Fifth Ego Center	respect / identity / recognition / choice / truth / a following / agreement
Sixth Ego Center	curiosity / engagement / effective foresight / persuasiveness / vision / good luck
Seventh Ego Center	ease / synchronicity / power / belonging / faith / resources / ecstasy / "miracles"

As you examine your Ego Centers, watch for places where one center may have tried to do the work that properly belongs to another. As children, we use what we can to thrive—or at least to survive—and our natural gifts and inclinations can lead us to favor one part of ourselves over others. For instance, some people give up their Second Ego Center need for pleasure and their Fourth Ego Center need for connection and value in order to secure their First Ego Center need for safety. Marrying for money is an example of this. Being stuck at a job you hate is another. If you weren't valued as a child—a Fourth Ego Center right—you may give away the gifts of other Ego Centers, such as wealth, sex, and choice, to acquire that feeling of value.

It is essential that each of your Ego Centers works clearly and effectively *in its own domain*, so they can all work together to give you their most successful and joyful expression in your life. That is not to say that, for example, a good love relationship can't also provide survival and safety. But if survival and safety come from giving up the needs of your Fourth Ego Center, you are perpetuating your injury. Your early caretakers were the only ones who should have provided those ego functions for you, and, even then, only until you were able to develop them for yourself. If you neglect to address distortions now, you will see the same challenges arising in all your adult relationships.

Identifying Ego Damage

You don't have to seek out your injuries or traumas. The minute you aim higher in any area of your existence, they are the first guests to the party. They are embedded in your patterns, and when you change those patterns, they take off their masks. As you reach for more in your life, they will increasingly present themselves in the form of obstacles, demanding that you address them so you can accomplish your goals. In my case, in order to function as a public speaker, I had to face the shame and fear my childhood had programmed into me and find tools and teachers to address those things. I didn't have to search for the underlying trauma; it showed itself when I reached for more. And any time I've moved forward in life, life itself has shown me where my old traumas were limiting me. At each such intersection, I could either choose to stay in the trauma-formed box I was in or get the tools I needed to do something else. I didn't have to make *resolving my trauma* the work; the limitations were simply indicators of what I needed help with.

Another example from my own life: As a child, my home's crazy was the crazy I knew. That meant I was poorly equipped for the normal world outside, where I didn't fit in as well. I spent my life thereafter creating safe and pleasant homes with people who mostly didn't have jobs or a place to belong, so they easily blended into my life. I didn't mind the extra burden that being the only functional person in the relationship entailed. But then I met the man who would one day become my second (and current) husband. He had a beautiful home of his own and a big career. That should have been great, right? Our relationship began with pure animal lust, but as I became involved with him, I was confronted with my own inherent resistance to moving out of my comfort zone and into someone else's. I found it extremely difficult to compromise in order to blend our lives. Which meant that my original trauma had to be confronted.

As synchronicity would have it, his ability to compromise was not the best either, and we both were presented with childhood patterns that we needed to heal. (It is something that we still work on.) Blood was spilled, but the relationship was important enough to both of us that we had a deep willingness to seek the tools of adaptation. That has positively impacted more than our relationship. Addressing these childhood patterns has allowed both of us to expand our work and put some boundaries on how others treat us.

Finding Your Focus

Although most of us know that something isn't quite right inside us, we sometimes have a hard time figuring out what the problem is and where it originated—our functional vulnerability. A quick way to locate its source is to notice where in your physical body you experience the most discomfort. Physical pain and illness often recur in the same place, and that can tell us something about our ego damage. Here is the key: *each Ego Center corresponds to one of the chakras that line the center of our bodies.* For example, those who struggle with their Fourth Ego Center, physically located at the heart, may experience poor heart health, while those with damage to their Sixth Ego Center, the "third eye," can suffer from chronic headaches.

Another approach is to identify the current challenges in your life and which Ego Center they correspond to. A partial list is provided in each chapter, but common sense will help you expand the list in a way that is unique to your structure.

If your current life challenge is that you do not have a home that you love, can afford, or that supports you, that is a First Ego Center challenge of foundation. Your attention may, however, go to something we cannot know, such as the fact that your living situation deteriorated after your husband left you, exposing a vulnerability of your Fourth Ego Center (self-worth). Extending the meaning of the Fourth Ego Center, you may find that focusing on healing how you value yourself in the absence of your ex may be the key to your healing. Your problem in finding friends or job opportunities may not be a Fourth Ego Center issue with connection. It may be that you don't correctly observe and evaluate your surroundings—in essence a mindfulness problem, which is your Sixth Ego Center. It sometimes helps to talk an issue through with someone who knows you well and can give you a sense of what they observe, a different perspective, to help you consider the nuance in your situation. As always, try the healing tools suggested for each Ego Center first. If you don't see change, consider which other centers may also be involved.

Here are a few questions to help you find your functional vulnerability. Answer as many as you can, and write your responses on a piece of paper or in a journal, so you can reference them easily.

- **If one thing could happen right now that would change your life, what would it be? What would it give you or restore in you?**

- **Where do you hurt? Literally, where in your physical body do you hurt? Put your hand there now. What Ego Center does that spot correspond to?**

- **What are your life's biggest challenges right now?**

- **What is your worst fear in this moment?**

- **What is your greatest failure or regret?**

- **Where do you lack balance?**

- **If you could choose one trait or habit to fix, what would it be?**

- **What power do you wish you had?**

- **What is the difficult emotion—shame, guilt, fear, regret— that most haunts you?**

- **Do you rely on others to provide something that you wish you could do for yourself?**

Now look at the previous charts and diagrams. Under which Ego Center do the majority of your challenges reside? There will be some crossover between the Ego Centers, but pick the most representative one.

Each time you do this exercise and explore its meaning, ask yourself this: "What do I have to do, *right now*, to create healing in the state of that Ego Center?" Try out some of the suggestions in the corresponding chapter. The way you'll know you've hit the right spot is that your life and your experience of life will change. Whenever it feels like life is working against you instead of with you, do this exercise to get clarity on where to place your efforts to be most effective in creating change.

As you read on, remember: You are not on earth to become more godlike. You are here to struggle with your humanity and your uniqueness. You are here to evolve spirit in the vehicle of your humanity and to evolve your ego by creating a joyful life. The increased accessibility of deep, unconflicted joy is the best indicator that you are doing your ego work.

You are unique. Your gifts are necessary to us all.

Final Preparation for the Work with Ego Centers

Next are some questions to consider for each Ego Center. Ask yourself these questions, but don't make this a ponderous process. You don't have to answer all the questions at once, and some may have no relevance to you. I offer them because creating new architecture sometimes requires drafting new plans, and these questions will help you create them. Get used to asking yourself these questions periodically, like a chorus, as needed.

In this moment:

- What are my goals?

- What is missing in my life?

- What is missing in my experience of life?

- What causes me pain?

- How do I want to serve the greater good?

- How do I need to be served by others?

- What do I want to heal?

- What are my superpowers?

- What do people want from me that I would rather not give?

- Did I skip a stage of development, or was one impaired? How might I introduce that experience now?

- How did my caretakers' experiences of each Ego Center in their own lives affect me?

- Whom did I rely on to meet the needs of each Ego Center?

- How did I adapt to these needs as I matured?

- How did I compensate for privation at injured Ego Centers?

- Did I take over the adult function of one or more of the Ego Centers too early?

The next set of questions addresses things that may happen, seemingly out of the blue, as you work with each Ego Center. Each Ego Center chapter is structured to give you a healing experience of the Ego Center it focuses on. Some Ego Centers may be very challenging and may even cause dramatic synchronicities that change your life. After you go through each chapter, pay close attention to the following:

- Is anything changing in your life?

- Who gets in touch with you?

- What obstacles appear?

- What offers appear out of the blue?

- How do your relationships to self, other, and world re-form?

- How does your experience of life change?

- Which memories come to consciousness to be reconciled?

- What are your dreams, and what issues and inspirations are your dreams leading you to?

- Does your physical appearance change?

- Does your health change?

- Do people react to you differently?

- Do you experience interactions differently?

It will be helpful to keep a journal to record how your efforts change your relationships, your experiences, your opportunities, even your body. These natural changes are the strongest indicators of where you need healing. You don't have to figure any of this out intellectually. An evidence-based practice like this one, in which you receive confirmation of your own efficacy very naturally, helps the subconscious embrace and integrate new beliefs, habits, and experiences. And that process broadens the possibilities for your life.

A Word of Advice as You Go Forward

Be flexible with your interpretation of each Ego Center. You are a unique being, and you have your own formula for existing. It may be helpful to refer to the descriptions of various functions at each Ego Center in the previous chapters to get an idea of what might change in your life as you work a particular Ego Center. The more you give yourself the message that you create your life through your actions and achievements, the more your subconscious and intuition will make change available to you. New opportunities will appear and, with them, new opportunities for healing.

You also may find that as you heal one Ego Center, another demands urgent attention. And that's fine. You can hop around and tend to the Ego Centers out of order. They work together and often in ways you may not recognize at first. In fact, where you think a block to your goals resides is often a red herring. The challenge to find love, for example, which you may think is a heart issue and therefore a matter of the Fourth Ego Center, may have roots in the injury of another underdeveloped Ego Center. Perhaps it's your inability to see clearly (Sixth Ego Center) that keeps you missing the people you could partner with, and you need to work on observation-intellect-intuition as a first step. Then you begin to see possible love connections but have trouble allowing your attractiveness to draw them to you (Second Ego Center). Once you deal with that, and you engage in an appropriate relationship, issues of trust may come up (Seventh Ego Center).

Of course, the way your own Ego Centers mesh with someone else's is also something to notice. Your own functional and open relationship to creativity, food, seduction, and sex (Second Ego Center) may be the strength you lead with, but the person you are attracted to may be initially open for connection only with someone who can first satisfy their need for a common future (Sixth Ego Center) and a solid foundation (First Ego Center). Such an awareness may help you grow in order to connect to another in ways that are enriching—or maybe exasperating, in which case you will probably choose someone else!

Often a path won't make sense to you, because it's a new path to a new outcome and *your old landmarks are gone.* The proof that you are on the right path lies in the results, even if those results are challenging at first. Anything new requires adjustment. Even receiving exactly what you ask for shakes up the old structure in a way that can sometimes be uncomfortable.

The first time I used the tools and did the exercises in this book, they changed me and my life dramatically. But it happened too fast to integrate the changes comfortably. I did all the work in two days and then took to my bed for a week, overwhelmed, as my life continued to alter around me. It was a productive experience but not a pleasant one. I suggest moderation and mindful pacing.

A Word of Explanation About the Tools That Conclude the Ego Center Chapters

At the end of each Ego Center chapter, you will find an intuitive tool and a healing tool. In some ways, they are like exercises; in some ways they are like meditations. I call them *tools* because that is what they are, useful ways to work with both ourselves and others and everything around us, all of which would be difficult to approach without them.

In most so-called self-help disciplines, tools provide ways to work on the self. That is not enough. The tools you will find here also provide practical approaches to "working the world"—other people, relationships, dynamics, events, objects, energies—the whole of creation. They are tools for change on both the micro and macro level, and in all points in time.

What is the difference between them?

An intuitive tool brings a dispassionate, almost objective understanding. It takes you a step back from subjectivity so that something can be seen anew and from any point in time and any perspective. A healing tool is almost mechanical; it restructures reality directly. Put in more concrete terms, the intuitive tool helps you see how you need to change the angles of your prism and the blueprint for the mechanics to do so. The healing tool gets you right into the act of change. Both are necessary to complete the job of re-creating your prism—your life and the structure of the world around you.

A Few Final Thoughts Before the Journey Begins

When you finish your first journey through this book, you will find yourself integrating the experience into not only your own life but also your guidance of others. I say "first journey" because life is a continual process of growth, achievement, maturing, and manifestation. A second passage through the book will yield further mastery. As it does, you will become a teacher.

Upon embarking on the Ego Center chapters, you may find their tone a little more challenging than that of the rest of the book. Those chapters have come to me this way, and I now realize there is a reason for that: they are like the spirit's dog whistle. They speak in a language you don't consciously recognize, a language that is the bridge between you and the you that is part of everything. Let these chapters enter you, even when you feel confused by them, even if you don't want to. Some of you will love their tone; others may find it about as pleasant as a bikini wax. It may make you want to kick a puppy or clip the wings of an angel. But let it work on you.

Something similar happened to me when I was writing my fourth book, *The Circle*. My hardheaded New Yorkness was completely at odds with the tenor of what was coming out of me, but it came out of me that way nevertheless. At the time, I was mystified. Then years later, I recorded the audiobook of *The Circle*, and to my surprise it got such a good response that I made myself sit down and listen to it—something I never do—and I saw what had happened. The book spoke in a voice that we cannot consciously hear. It was like the call of a siren's song. Its language, I realized, was the secret handshake that allows us into the real work.

So let the tone of these chapters enter you, even if it triggers the kinds of judgments that it triggered in me. The important thing to notice is what changes in your life when you work an Ego Center chapter as it is intended. Tools work whether or not you enjoy using them—or even believe in them.

Change demands courage and an absolute commitment to act as consciously as possible. Work through your emotional challenges by not allowing them to stop you and by employing everything at your disposal—dreams, therapy, groups, journaling, and all other guides to your hidden world. Make every time zone useful. Let all your memories become the tools for your alchemic transformation. Awareness is the key.

You are now the adult. You are now your own parent, caretaker, and teacher. You now have agency that you didn't have as a young child.

You also have us—*all* of us—the other projections of spirit that are working with you, as you are working with them. Together, we will reengineer your inner architecture. Suspend the illusion of separateness. We are all working together because, at the most essential level, we are one.

The real work begins now . . .

Exercise

RECALIBRATING THE PRISM

Before reading each of the following Ego Center chapters, have your coin bag ready.

1. Pick a coin, but don't look at it.

2. Write down the numbers 1 through 7 on a piece of paper or in a journal and quickly—without giving yourself time to think, reason, or get creative—write a word (or two) for each number. Write whatever comes to mind: a noun, an adjective, a person, a memory, an image, a song title. Allow your intuition a full range to express itself.

3. When you finish the chapter, look at the goal associated with the coin you picked, and notice how these "word symbols" guided you to a new way to use the Ego Center you were working on.

7

Your First Ego Center

The higher your structure is to be,
the deeper must be its foundation.

—SAINT AUGUSTINE

CORRESPONDS TO: THE ROOT CHAKRA

LOCATION: BASE OF THE SPINE

Caretakers Represent Safe Structure
and Foundation

Birth	Development	Maturity
SURVIVAL	COMPETENCE	POWER

This Ego Center corresponds to whether you feel safe and supported in the world. It governs your power to create wealth and other structures of security in your surroundings and your ability to defend what is yours against disruptive and destructive influences. It is your power to affect the world and to build and inhabit a world where you and others thrive.

Properties of the First Ego Center

Life Phase: Birth: You are born with the right to exist.

Life Phase: Development: You are tasked with the development of competence.

Life Phase: Maturity: You earn the gift of power.

Ego Defense: dissociation/distraction

Ego Challenge: self-support

Ego Wound: isolation

Ego Strength: sanctuary

Place of Joy: order

Polarity: structure vs. flexibility

Physical Gift: presence

Spiritual Gift: remote viewing/astral projection

Rehabilitation/Healing: absolute attention to healthy structures and disciplines

Life Phase: **Birth**

SURVIVAL

Birthright: *You are born with the right to exist.*

You were born into circumstances that determined how secure you would be in life, how powerfully alive you would be, and also what distortions you would incorporate into this Ego Center in order to survive.

For your First Ego Center to be able to mature into its full power, the following statements needed to be true early in your development (from birth through infancy).

Your caretakers provided you with a secure place in the world.

Your parents willingly made space in their lives for your arrival and affirmed your presence right from the start.

Your caretakers felt that they were safe and that they could keep you safe.

When you were an infant, your demands were met and structures were in place to assure your safety and health.

Routines were reliable.

You were born healthy and did not have to struggle with undue discomfort. If you struggled with discomfort, you had caretakers who made those challenges manageable.

When there were challenges to your safety or routine, you were firmly anchored in the protection afforded by your caretakers.

You felt secure enough to express your presence.

Your siblings were prepared for your birth and welcomed you into the family. If children were born after you, your place in the family changed in a way that was manageable and rewarding.

Life Phase: **Development**

COMPETENCE

You are tasked with the development of competence.

What was done for you as a baby you gradually learned to do for yourself. You were supported in gaining autonomy while developing your individuality.

For your First Ego Center to be able to mature into its full power, the following statements needed to be true in your first six or seven years of life.

As you learned the tasks of self-mastery—crawling, grappling, sitting up, standing, walking—you were celebrated and encouraged.

You were given safe boundaries and clear discipline, enabling you to explore your world and try out your new skills in safety.

As you grew, your place in the family was clear and secure. If other children were born after you, you were helped to find your place in the new order and did not feel displaced.

When you went to school, you had teachers who liked you and you made friends with your peers.

Your home life was settled enough to allow you to develop as an individual and learn how to navigate the world beyond your home.

Even when faced with challenges in the family (divorce, illness, geographical moves, difficulties at school, etc.), you were able to cope and maintain a secure place in your family. The adults around you provided firm grounding during these changes.

Your caretakers helped you to safely tolerate discomfort until you were old enough to distract yourself by focusing on what you could achieve in the moment.

Dissociation, your First Ego Center defense, was engaged only if you were exposed to information that was overwhelming or pain that was unbearable. Ideally, you dissociated for only a short time and it provided enough distance from the pain to allow you to function.

Your caretakers encouraged your autonomy in the world and supported you when your efforts at self-sufficiency fell short. You grew up with a sense of being a competent and able person.

You were able to create sanctuary for yourself and those around you no matter where you were.

You found common ground and goals in your peer group.

Life Phase: Maturity

POWER

You earn the gift of power.

Having integrated the formula for survival and the ability to find autonomy and competence in any situation, you developed the quality of power.

If your First Ego Center has been able to mature into its full power, the seeds of the following statements—along with the successful foundation work of the birth and development phases—will be true:

> As you matured, you secured an education, a peer group, a group of mentors to guide you, a job, sufficient wealth and resources, a secure place to live, and other elements of a solid and protected existence.

> You have been able to respond to and move on from the temporary, inevitable setbacks of life. When people or situations have undermined your well-being, you have been quick and skillful in removing yourself from them.

> You acquire the rules for success in every situation.

> You have an instinctual aversion to anything that challenges your safety, allowing you to be courageous and secure in taking calculated, profitable risks.

> You have been consistently able to find a home for your talents. They have been rewarded monetarily and emotionally.

> Inevitably, there have been moments when things didn't work out as you planned, but your sense of self was strong enough to allow you to move forward and build something even better and more appropriate from these setbacks.

> If you partnered in life, whether for love or business, you found someone trustworthy and useful.

> At some point, you became comfortable enough to provide for others in your life—financially, emotionally, and professionally.

You have experienced and provided both sanctuary and belonging.

When you die, your affairs will be in order and set up to sustain future generations. You transition into death with a sense of safety, satisfaction, and belonging.

Ego Defense: Dissociation/Distraction

When the First Ego Center is challenged, the response is often dissociating, or detaching from reality. Your mind no longer feels like a part of your body as you separate from intolerable stimuli. When you are a child, this First Ego Center defense is engaged only if you are exposed to overwhelming information or unbearable pain. The ability to temporarily dissociate from injurious stimuli can be protective, but extended periods of dissociation can lead to lasting damage to the First Ego Center. A more mature response is the ability to distract appropriately while dealing with both the needs of self and the demands of the environment. In so doing, you engage your ability to choose your focus and/or mitigate the injurious experience without abandoning yourself.

Ego Challenge: Self-Support

The challenge of the First Ego Center is to find elements of support within yourself and in your environment. The support and structure you experience early on teaches you to find an inner order and confidence that attracts the same in your life. When, later in life, that support fails, your early experience allows you to identify and develop new sources of support. If your First Ego Center is injured, you may struggle to support yourself in some areas of your life. Your finances and health may reflect this struggle. When your First Ego Center is healed, it will provide you with the ability to attract, demand, create, and sustain the support you need in order to live a comfortable life.

Ego Wound: Isolation

At birth, you emerge from a physical unity with your mother. When you enter the world, you are meant to be part of another safe structure that includes your caretakers, your community, and your environment. If this transition is not made safely, you experience the trauma of isolation. When this isolation continues through your early development, you won't know how to look for your place of belonging. You create ersatz protective structures that never reach the level of integration with the larger world.

Ego Strength: Sanctuary

A healthy First Ego Center is able to find order and breathe vitality into any situation to create a safe haven for self and others, even during times of upheaval. This power reflects a profound sense of belonging. "Haven't we all got a garden inside?" was a line in a poem I wrote at fourteen after the suicide of my mother. I can now go to any country and find my home and my people.

Place of Joy: Order

The First Ego Center thrives in an atmosphere of order, structure, and predictability. Healthy routines create security, allowing you to respond effectively to the demands of life and create the future you want. An inadequately structured First Ego Center will become the

Achilles' heel of any achievement; it's like depending on shifting sands for support. An afflicted First Ego Center often seeks order by embracing dogma—or rejects order completely, creating crises that may feel like structure but are shaky, artificial, and very transitory. When a healthy structure is found and adhered to, the "terra firma" it provides gives you a springboard toward freedom, expansion, and greatness.

Polarity: Structure vs. Flexibility

A healthy, mature First Ego Center needs flexibility as well as structure to thrive. Once a firm, reliable foundation is in place, this Ego Center can adapt to new circumstances, reach higher, and safely soften routines. You can "take off" only if you have a solid base to do it from, and you can do that safely only if you have the ability to create organized and adaptive new systems. You don't want to be so structured that you are rigid and cannot expand, nor so flexible that you are bent and twisted by the world around you. A healthy First Ego Center allows you to stay the course while being flexible enough to grow, adapt, and maintain a smoothly ordered life.

Physical Gift: Presence

The physical gift of a strong First Ego Center is presence. When your First Ego Center is healthy and functional, your very presence— your being—creates success, not just in your own life but in the world around you. You walk into a room, a job, or a relationship, and your power and vitality enhance the situation. You are welcome, acknowledged, and in your element. You are rewarded, even celebrated, for existing because your presence is alchemic.

Spiritual Gift:
Remote Viewing/Astral Projection

You engage in astral projection and remote viewing all the time without being consciously aware of it. Astral projection is the ability to energetically be in more than one place at the same time. You are, in fact, never 100 percent in one place. Remote viewing is the ability to perceive another location. When you observe another location, you are remote viewing. When you experience and interact with that location, you are astral projecting.

These abilities maintain your connection to a larger world, but they also demand energy that can prevent you from being effective in your present reality. As you refine your command of this ability, you will "travel" only when you need to find information or impact something remotely, and your awareness will enhance your mastery of the present.

Notice, for a moment, where you have been traveling in your mind's eye as you have been reading this chapter. It might be to another room in your house or to where a loved one is, to a place in your past, or even to a place you have not yet seen. Now fully inhabit that place with your senses. Allow yourself to describe it in detail and, as you do, experience it more and more as if you were there. When you feel the juxtaposition of where you are physically and where you are energetically, you may feel comfortable enough to engage with people or objects in that other environment.

You also may want to verify your observations and notice the effects of your interactions. For example, if you see someone you care about in a place you are "visiting," interact with them, engaging as many senses as possible. Notice if they call you or continue in another way the contact that you engaged in when you were "with" them. The more that you can verify the perceptions and impacts resulting from these interactions, the more your intellect and subconscious will use this skill to negotiate your everyday life.

Rehabilitation/Healing: Absolute Attention to Healthy Structures and Disciplines

The rehabilitation of the First Ego Center is focused on discipline and devotion to what is life-sustaining and a strict avoidance of what is dangerous. It is what I call "taking care of the mammal." Discipline is the ability to structure energy and resources to meet present needs and future goals. This is not a rigid, punitive discipline but the loving support and structure of consistent self-care, though it is not always clear-cut what that is. For example, you may need to save money for a project instead of spending it on a massage, even though the massage seems more grounding in the moment. You may need to distance yourself from a friendship that makes you happy but makes your life more chaotic. Choosing in favor of your own stability may be new for you, and initially it can even be unsatisfying until you see the stunning gifts it brings. The "no new damage" rule is the healer of the First Ego Center. If there is a potential for a situation to bring new damage to your life, think twice.

This rule is especially urgent in times of change. When your foundation is threatened, or the constellations around you shift, or the elements you need in order to be competent change in a way that you are not yet equipped to handle, doing only what is healthy, productive, and life-sustaining will see you through to solid ground. During times when the First Ego Center is unable to recognize the terrain, it needs to open its receptors to the most basic feedback loops of life: food, shelter, connection, rest, activity, purpose, and safety. Then the new terrain will eventually reveal itself, and you will have maintained your safety until then. This often requires a temporary dissociation from outside events and the feelings they bring forth in favor of simple functioning.

Injured Development of the First Ego Center

Answer the questions that follow honestly to understand what might have interfered with the healthy use and development of your First Ego Center. At the end of this chapter, you will find an exercise to help heal injured First Ego Centers.

1. Were you born into a family in which your own survival was in jeopardy?

2. Was there violence in your home?

3. Were your parents unable to find a supportive community?

4. Did you belong to a marginalized racial, gender, ethnic, or socioeconomic group?

5. Did you have to take care of your own safety, structure, and supervision before you were developmentally competent enough to do so?

6. Was your birth unplanned and unwelcome?

7. Were you criticized for age-appropriate needs for support?

8. Were you brutally disciplined, either physically or verbally?

9. Were mistakes in your efforts toward autonomy, such as spilling something or dressing yourself inexpertly, punished?

10. Were you abandoned in significant ways, whether by circumstance or by neglectful parenting?

11. Did you have to make yourself invisible for your own safety?

12. Were you overindulged and/or shielded from normal developmental challenges and consequences?

13. Were you unable or not expected to follow the rules of home, society, or school?

14. Were you exposed to developmentally inappropriate information that disrupted your sense of safety?

15. Were you genetically wired for anxiety?

16. Did you have an illness that put your life at risk or made it uncomfortable to be in your body?

17. Were you raised with emotionally disordered people who did not provide safe structures in which to thrive?

Signs of an Afflicted First Ego Center

If you answered yes to any of the above "Injured Development" questions about your childhood, you may experience the following challenges in your adult life:

You have a hard time finding a safe place—a home for yourself—in the world.

You are unable to create stability for yourself in the world.

You feel as if you aren't really here and alive.

You are detached from your own needs and experiences.

You have a hard time supporting yourself and unconsciously reject the support of others.

You compulsively take care of others while never getting your own needs met.

Although you live with abundance, you often feel that it can be taken from you at any time or that it's not enough.

You feel pressured to enter or remain in an unsatisfying marriage/job/community to meet your support needs.

You are dissociated from your feelings, hunger, pleasures, or relationships. You have a hard time experiencing the moment or even the passage of time.

You feel or are treated as if you are invisible or inconsequential.

The Results of a Misdirected First Ego Center

- poverty in any area of life

- anxiety, panic, and/or terror

- a lack of supportive structures in your work, relationships, or community

- physical issues concerning structure, flexibility, or support

- isolation and a sense of not belonging

- uncontainable rage

- hard labor or devotion/sacrifice without reward

- lack of access to life-sustaining resources or the tendency to give them away inappropriately or have them stolen from you

- homelessness in fact or experience

How to Heal the First Ego Center

- Absolute attention to what is life-sustaining.

- No New Damage.

- Absolute avoidance of debilitating or dangerous people, situations, or practices.

- Knowing and following the rules.

- Choosing grounded, solid, stable people, habits, and behaviors.

- Positive, realistic thinking.

- Keeping your attention on the "can do" in a situation.

- Discipline and routine.

- Keeping up with obligations.

Focus on these grounding behaviors and nurture the parts of yourself that seek stability. From that basis, an afflicted First Ego Center can truly begin to grow and heal. If you don't actively work on such rehabilitation, you risk missing the sometimes-daunting opportunities that require real change, and you will become too inflexible and scattered to properly integrate new, healthy structures, opportunities, and relationships into your life.

Healing Questions

It is helpful to write down your responses to these questions and update them as you do the work in this book.

1. Am I upholding my responsibilities to myself and others?

2. Am I adhering to healthy physical, psychological, financial, relational, and nutritional routines and disciplines?

3. Where in my life do I experience chaos?

4. Where do I have power in my life?

5. What cues tell me when I am safe/unsafe, and how can I distance myself from the people and situations that make me feel unsafe?

6. What people, activities, and achievements create more stability in my life?

7. Where in my life do I lose or give away my power?

8. Where am I overly rigid and unable to adapt?

9. How can I make my living/working environment support my well-being and goals?

10. What disciplines would allow me to make headway toward fulfilling my desires and goals?

11. When do I feel most healthy and at home?

When You Heal Your First Ego Center

- You attract recognition and security in all areas of your life.

- You intuitively avoid dangerous people and situations without the need for hypervigilance.

- You feel "at home" and that your needs are met.

- You are consistently surrounded by safe structures—a good job, a secure home, a healthy relationship, supportive communities.

- You are resilient and supported when there are challenges.

- You experience a sense of vitality and well-being.

- Income, relationships, community, and work are no longer arduous but sources of joy and support. You notice new opportunities to improve your standing in the world—a new job, new home, better relationships.

- Change, even trauma, consistently takes you to a better, safer, and more abundant place.

- You take appropriate risks with significant rewards.

- Your life has a new sense of ease as meeting your needs and desires becomes an organic result of your effective functioning.

Daily Assertions

I am a safe foundation.

My mistakes are growth.

I am perfectly imperfect.

I have a right to exist.

Fear guides me to safety.

I have the power to change my life.

I can support myself.

I am irreplaceable.

I strive to be a safe person for others and myself.

My choices ensure that past failures lead to future successes.

I attract the resources I need by being my most grounded self.

I have not mastered everything . . . yet.

What is mine belongs to me.

I belong.

INTUITIVE TOOL FOR THE
FIRST EGO CENTER

Pick one of your coins. Don't look at it.

Take a moment to notice where your mind is. You will find that it isn't here in the room, in the present moment with you; it is elsewhere.

Now allow your full attention and your senses to be in that other place. Don't close your eyes—this place is not imaginary. Create a sensory experience of being in that other place. Who is there? What is around you? You can choose to participate in the activity that is occurring there. Notice the reactions of the other people present. If you participate, you may notice that the people you interact with will continue that interaction in real time, hours, days, or even weeks later.

Now look at the coin. Notice what this experience illuminated about the goal you picked.

We often visit the past or future or even someone else's reality without being consciously aware of it. When your attention is elsewhere, it is likely that you are traveling in time or space, to a location other than where your body is now. This is a skill we often don't recognize, and it can be very useful for gathering information, resolving issues from the past, or reprogramming the future. However, consider this: You can make real change only in the present moment. The more you dissociate from this moment, the less powerful and secure you are. It is important to have some control when you are partially "out of your body" as well as when you more fully inhabit your power.

Now pick another coin. Don't look at it.

This time, do the reverse. Again, follow your attention to all the places where you "are" in your mind's eye, but bring yourself back to reality by focusing on experiencing where you are now. Notice each one of your senses as it perceives this point in space-time, this moment, this now.

Every time your senses and attention wander, bring them back. If you do this regularly, you will have a much greater impact on the situations and interactions you are physically in.

Now look at the coin. Notice what this experience illuminated about the goal you picked.

HEALING TOOL FOR THE
FIRST EGO CENTER

To begin, ask yourself (and then answer!) the following questions:

- Where is your life limited?

- Where does it feel out of control?

Now imagine you are enrolled at Life University. What lesson plan have you been given based on your answers to the two questions above? And if a specific situation is forcing you to learn, change, and/or adapt, what would you do right now to address it? If your life is chaotic or you face a seemingly unattainable goal, what is being demanded of you?

At first, your responses may include only a few activities, such as striking up a conversation with one new person a day if you're looking for a relationship, or spending twenty minutes a day learning a new skill, or taking on some freelance work if you aren't making enough money. Once you start doing these things reliably and consistently, add more. Choose structures that support your goals. The First Ego Center rewards practical action.

Pick only a few challenges to start with and apply this remedy consistently. Dramatic shifts from tiny changes are most available at the First Ego Center because it's the foundation for your entire life. I suggest you keep a record of what changes and how to begin developing your own rule book for miracles.

The First Ego Center craves structure and reliability, but it also demands flexibility. If you are inflexible by nature, you must actively try to respond adaptively to the surprises that come your way. How might this situation be guiding you in the right direction? How could you respond in a new way? Whom do you know who manages the same situation well? How could you mirror that behavior? Seek to create a new, healthy structure in which your First Ego Center can thrive instead of trying (and failing) to maintain the now-useless structure you relied on before.

Whether this is your first healing of the First Ego Center or you have returned to this chapter more than once, you will notice that each time you go through these exercises, your life becomes more secure. You are presented with opportunities to become more competent and are rewarded for competencies you already have, and you are empowered and supported in reaching your goals by the world around you.

You are home. You are welcome. Your presence creates both those things.

8

Your Second Ego Center

Many of us pursue pleasure with such breathless
haste that we hurry past it.

—Søren Kierkegaard

CORRESPONDS TO: THE SEXUAL CHAKRA
LOCATION: JUST BELOW THE NAVEL

Caretakers Represent Nourishment and Boundaries

Birth	Development	Maturity
NOURISHMENT	CREATIVITY	ABUNDANCE

This Ego Center controls your ability to share in a healthy way and experience pleasure. It is also directly related to your ability to be a semipermeable membrane, keeping toxins out while letting nourishment in. It governs your attractiveness in all areas and your ability to be uniquely you in a way that is healthy, functional, fun, and rewarded by the world.

Properties of the Second Ego Center

Life Phase: Birth: You have the right to nourishment.

Life Phase: Development: You are tasked with the development of creativity.

Life Phase: Maturity: You earn the gift of abundance.

Ego Defense: regression

Ego Challenge: gratitude

Ego Wound: gluttony

Ego Strength: evolution

Place of Joy: creativity

Polarity: porosity vs. boundaries

Physical Gift: attraction

Spiritual Gift: mediumship

Rehabilitation/Healing: pleasure

Life Phase: **Birth**

NOURISHMENT

Birthright: *You have the right to nourishment.*

Your second right as a physical being is your right to thrive. Long before nourishment and protection became developmental tasks, your caretakers and environment created both strengths and distortions in this Ego Center.

For your Second Ego Center to be able to mature into its full power, most of the following statements needed to be true early in your development (from birth through infancy).

Your birth delighted your caretakers and siblings.

Your family had sufficient resources to share with you when you were born.

When your family encountered challenges, you were appropriately shielded from them.

Your early emotional, psychosocial, and physical needs were met.

If your needs could not be met, your caretakers found other ways to nourish you.

Your caretakers were able to nurture each other.

Your caretakers were part of a supportive community.

Your caretakers had the capacity to experience and share joy.

Nourishing you was a source of pleasure for the people around you, and your growth was celebrated.

Your nourishment was unconditional and free of your caretakers' personal agendas and expectations.

The adults around you created a secure boundary between you and danger and between you and your own dangerous impulses.

Life Phase: **Development**

CREATIVITY

You are tasked with the development of creativity.

As you strived for autonomy, your ability to find and create what you needed became a developmental task.

For your Second Ego Center to be able to mature into its full power, the seeds of the following statements needed to be true in your first six or seven years of life.

As you learned how to self-soothe, you found ways to comfort yourself and delay gratification without feeling deprived.

Issues around toilet training were dealt with in a supportive way.

You were encouraged to develop a sense of security and privacy around your "private parts" and "private functions," along with a feeling of being able to address your own needs.

When you went to school, you were rewarded for exhibiting appropriate social behavior.

If other siblings were born after you, you remained a priority for your caretakers and continued to be rewarded for age-appropriate development.

You developed the ability to discern the difference between appropriate risks and real dangers.

Your failures were experienced as seeds of your future success.

You acknowledged failure without shame, and appropriate shame was met with opportunities for redemption.

As you developed into a sexual being, you were given adequate privacy, protection, and a set of self-preserving boundaries that ensured that your psychosexual experiences were in keeping with your development.

You easily learned how to identify and leave situations and relationships that were toxic.

Punishment was appropriate and understood as corrective.

Your creations, whether a drawing or a poop in the potty, were met with encouragement and celebration.

You were taught that creating joy for others was a personal success.

Rules, limits, and boundaries that were too mature for you to integrate were clear and reliably maintained for you.

When old sources of nourishment and comfort became obsolete, you discovered new ones.

Life Phase: Maturity

ABUNDANCE

You earn the gift of abundance.

When one is properly nourished for healthy growth and has developed the ability to find and create from what is available, the natural result is abundance. In the energy of abundance, resources flow easily, and you choose what is useful and what is not. From these experiences you create and attract what you need for your unique version of life. Your presence creates this dynamic for others.

If your Second Ego Center has been able to mature into its full power, the seeds of the following statements—along with the successful foundation work of the birth and development phases—will be true:

As you moved into adulthood, you integrated in your own life the boundaries your parents modeled. You know to avoid disordered people, dangerous situations, and risky behaviors, such as drug and alcohol abuse, while maintaining a healthy routine.

Your own individual lens on the world has added to your professional success.

You have used creative outlets to express yourself and find the pleasure hidden in even the most challenging moments.

You have built satisfying relationships with others, which has given you the fuel to do and be more in your own life.

If you started a family, you find that fulfilling your partner's and your children's needs is rewarding. You are also able to support those in need in your community in a meaningful way.

The inevitable times of loneliness, loss, illness, and creative frustration have ultimately resulted in a greater ability to nourish and express yourself.

You respect your limitations and recognize when you can challenge them safely.

You accept care and support from appropriate sources.

You recognize and repel dangerous situations and people.

With your experience of abundance, you can delay gratification, knowing it will come.

People and resources are attracted to you.

Death is the natural evolution of your life, and you will experience it with meaning and comfort. You will transition joyfully, knowing that what you need always awaits you and what you leave is a unique creation that will inspire others.

Ego Defense: Regression

When your Second Ego Center is injured, you regress to (or consistently inhabit) a less mature stage of development. You lose the ability to regulate, protect, and direct your own drives, emotions, needs, and nourishment, leaving you open to self-destructive behaviors and exploitation by others. Once you begin to heal this Ego Center, you will learn to recognize the conditions that cause regression, such as hunger, too little sleep, exposure to trauma triggers, or too much/little stimulation. You will be able to address them and comfort yourself in more sophisticated and creative ways.

Ego Challenge: Gratitude

The Second Ego Center regulates desire and the hunger that drives you to leave your comfort zone, seeking appropriate nourishment for growth. Although this is the energy that impels you to evolve, it can also impede you from using and enjoying what you've attained. Gratitude—acknowledging your own achievements—brings pleasure and the energy for further growth.

Ego Wound: Gluttony

When you want more of something beyond its usefulness, you are in the wound of the Second Ego Center. Devoid of gratitude, stuck in an old experience of hunger, or compensating for the privation of another Ego Center, you will be driven by gluttony to acquire, experience, and ingest so much that what was once a need or joy becomes an element of dysfunction, even corruption, in your life.

Ego Strength: Evolution

The Second Ego Center is home to our organs of maturity and procreation. Evolution requires that we shed or integrate an old identity in order to embrace new growth. It brings to the future only what serves, leaving behind the structures that hold us back. The baby becomes a child, the child a woman, the woman a mother, and so on in the cycle of growth. This Ego Center nourishes thoughts, ideas, projects, and goals that bring the best experiences to each new cycle.

Place of Joy: Creativity

When you have a healthy Second Ego Center, you will find joy in creating what you (and others) need and desire. At its most empowered, this creative capacity will allow you to take from life what is necessary while filtering out toxicity. Someone with an afflicted Second Ego Center will use this same drive to get their perceived needs met but in manipulative ways that are injurious to self and others.

Polarity: Porosity vs. Boundaries

The Second Ego Center functions as both fodder and filter for our nourishment and pleasure. You need to be open enough to receive from outside sources of growth and pleasure but maintain adequate boundaries to protect yourself from harm. While being nourished, you may experience trouble keeping your boundaries and respecting the boundaries of others. When you give, you may do so with hidden and/or mutually destructive secondary agendas. You may be oblivious to others' very appropriate boundaries, or you may allow situations where others exercise inappropriate entitlement to your resources and being.

The boundaries that allow us to identify toxicity—in ourselves and others—are vitally important for our own abundance and satisfaction. Maintaining the balance between the polarities of receptivity and self-protection is the lifelong—and often challenging—task of the Second Ego Center. What you might appropriately give to a child, for example, is not the same as what you would give to a friend or even a spouse. Your desire to feed yourself—nutritionally, sexually, socially, or in any other way—requires that you also manage your limits.

Physical Gift: Attraction

A secure Second Ego Center radiates attractiveness. Others will sense that you have nourishment, joy, and pleasure to offer them. Your energy will enrich and add comfort to any situation. You will benefit from the attention and care of others. They will take pleasure in and applaud your creativity. Your *being*—not what you do—will draw resources toward you. A healthy Second Ego Center maintains the boundaries that protect your attractiveness from unwanted intrusions and demands. There is a healthy entitlement to getting your needs met before taking on others' needs.

Spiritual Gift: Mediumship

Can you recall a time when you not only knew what someone was feeling but experienced that knowledge overtaking your own sense of self? Have you ever unconsciously behaved the way someone else wanted you to? Embodying the experiences and wishes of others and seeing things from their point of view is an aspect of mediumship. The distinction between you and others is, like the distinction between your current self and past and future selves, surprisingly insubstantial. This is why those of us with Second Ego Center challenges must actively seek out pleasure. Without enough pleasure, you will use your natural ability to merge with others to escape the hunger and pain of your damaged Second Ego Center. This is a full-on sensory experience of dissociation from your own individual self—an unhealthy mental state to inhabit.

When employed with intention and care, mediumship can give you vital information about situations, people, and even companies that you want to know more about. But if you have a natural tendency toward merging/mediumship, maintain an awareness of it—it will help you stay true to yourself when you are helping others. If you are taking a position on an issue or making a decision, be conscious of whether your mind is inhabiting someone else's point of view. If you remain present in your own healthy Second Ego Center, you will be able to filter out toxicity and approach situations with clarity.

Rehabilitation/Healing: Pleasure

The Second Ego Center is fed by pleasure as it expands your experience of gratification with every stage of its growth and discovery. Pleasure is not something the world gives us but something we find within and then apply to our experience. When you look for the pleasure and nourishment in every situation—even the most mundane or outwardly unpleasant—you find your power, opportunities for growth, and the solace to respond with maturity.

Injured Development of the Second Ego Center

Answer the questions that follow honestly to understand what might have interfered with the healthy use and development of your Second Ego Center. At the end of this chapter, you will find an exercise to help heal injured Second Ego Centers.

1. Were you born into a family where you felt there wasn't enough to go around?

2. Did you feel like a burden on the resources of your family? Did your caregivers need to make drastic sacrifices in order to feed/nourish you?

3. Did your caretakers demand that you feed them emotionally in inappropriate or smothering ways?

4. Were there dietary practices in your home that you perceived as punitive or restrictive?

5. Was there enough appropriate emotional touch and support?

6. Were your physical and/or sexual boundaries violated? Were you allowed privacy?

7. Were you expected to self-regulate, self-contain, and self-comfort at too early an age, as in premature toilet training or not having appropriate needs met in a timely way?

8. Were you shamed because of your needs or difficulties?

9. Were you expected to care for other people at an inappropriately early age? Did you constantly have to put your needs aside for others?

10. Were you shamed or ridiculed for sometimes falling back into immature behaviors such as toileting accidents, meltdowns, or needing your baby blanket or stuffed animals?

11. Were you babied by overprotective or controlling parents?

12. Did you have a child before you reached maturity?

13. Did you have to care for an ill or disturbed parent?

14. Did you lose a parent at a young age?

15. Did your caretakers use you to fill their own intimacy needs? Was there inappropriate sharing of feelings?

Signs of an Afflicted Second Ego Center

If you answered yes to any of the above "Injured Development" questions about your childhood, you may experience the following challenges in your adult life:

You have a hard time attracting enough resources to do what you want to do. Others are rewarded for their efforts, but you don't seem to have the knack. Even when you do well, certain people and situations drain your assets.

You are not aware of your needs, or you fight them in order to control them, as happens with eating disorders or codependence.

You struggle with your weight and never feel full. You continually try to soothe yourself with food and are prone to addictions. Conversely, you may be wary of nourishment and growth and try to control your environment by limiting nourishment in dangerous and even obsessive ways.

You are unable to experience joy, satisfaction, or pleasure.

You have wealth but carry around a sense of emptiness.

You have a hard time protecting your boundaries, financially, emotionally, physically, sexually, or psychically.

You feel that you aren't worthwhile unless you are supporting or caring for someone else.

You have a hard time being alone and valuing yourself.

You isolate yourself and feel that you cannot or do not get anything of real value from others.

You fall in love with people who cannot or will not nourish and support you or who fail to commit to you in other important ways.

You are shackled to a job that doesn't allow your creativity or uniqueness to be expressed.

You are goal oriented without ever taking pleasure from your achievements.

You are afraid of getting older because you haven't fulfilled many of your dreams, and you cling to an inappropriately youthful life or appearance.

You feel an inordinate amount of shame over your basic needs or simple mistakes.

The Results of a Misdirected Second Ego Center

* eating, sexual, addictive, and self-harming disorders

* privation

* lack of support for projects, relationships, and goals

* victimization

* picking abusive partners or partners who don't meet your needs

* shame

* blame

* envy

* inability to experience joy and pleasure

* perceiving yourself as unattractive or making yourself unattractive

* hunger

* joylessness

How to Heal the Second Ego Center

- Seek out healthy pleasures.

- Pay attention to boundaries with others and self.

- Moderate habits of both excess and restriction.

- Be creative.

- Weed out costly friendships, behaviors, and neuroses.

- Maintain a healthy diet.

- Nourish all the senses through arts and sensual pleasures.

- Use self-soothing techniques such as exercise, meditation, breath work, self-pleasuring, and experiencing nature.

- Seek out and create comfort and pleasure.

- Increase your tolerance for discomfort where the reward is significant.

- Notice areas of "hunger" in your life and implement a plan to address them.

- Use discipline to allocate time and energy for creative and productive activities.

- Use every challenge as an opportunity to create.

Healing Questions

It is helpful to write down your responses to these questions and update them as you do the work in this book.

1. How can I give myself some pleasure or relief right now, at this moment? (Now do it!)

2. What is my creative outlet, and how can I integrate it into my life (right now)?

3. Where am I physically or emotionally uncomfortable, and how can I limit my exposure to this discomfort?

4. When do I say yes when I mean no?

5. How can I say no more effectively?

6. How can I ask for more pleasure in my relationships?

7. What do I need to change to be comfortable with my sexuality and sexual relationship(s)?

8. How can I better nourish myself?

9. What can I do to replace unhealthy habits (starting now, in small ways)?

10. How can I replace shame with awareness and a commitment to growth?

When You Heal Your Second Ego Center

- Supportive people surround you.

- You attract wealth and abundance in all areas of your life.

- You have profuse creativity.

- You experience joy in all areas of your life.

- Although you are able to be generous with others, you take care of yourself first without guilt or shame.

- You have strong boundaries.

- You are able to process the past without shame. Having learned from your mistakes, you feel accomplished.

- If you have struggled with binge eating (or obsessive restriction), you can now recognize satiety and enjoy it.

- If you have struggled with sexuality or infertility, you find solutions.

- Your sex life is healthy and satisfying.

- You easily experience pleasure even when life isn't perfect.

- You have no addictions.

- What you desire nourishes you.

- Whom you desire nourishes you.

- You can say no gracefully and definitively when you need to.

Daily Assertions

I am enough.

I create beauty, and the beauty I create creates abundance for me.

My mistakes are my teachers.

I am a dynamic work in progress.

I have an obligation to protect my body, mind, and spirit.

I forgive myself, and I am forgiven.

I do my best, and when it falls short, I learn to do better.

Abundance fills me when I release all attachment to those who have harmed me.

Pleasure is mine to discover.

I can provide myself with a safe space when I need to regress and find nourishment and comfort from the old and familiar.

When I remove toxins, I make space for nourishment.

I am not responsible for the needs or feelings of others.

Toxic situations and habits are resolved through my commitment to pleasure and nourishment.

No shame, no blame.

When I say no, I act on no.

I don't have to be worthy to receive.

INTUITIVE TOOL FOR THE SECOND EGO CENTER

For this simple mediumship exercise, we will practice with an inanimate object. Later, when you become more skilled (and healed) in your Second Ego Center, you can consciously inhabit other people and past and future selves. And as with most of the exercises in this book, you will be using your mediumship skills to get more information about one of your goals.

1. First, pick one of your coins (but don't look at it).

2. What tree, flower, animal, scent, person, or object comes to mind?

3. Become it. Speak from its experience using the first person.

4. When you inhabit the thing you have chosen, what does it feel like to be you? Experience yourself with all your senses.

5. When you are this thing, look outward. Perceive from yourself and know where you are.

6. Who is around you?

7. Where are you in time? Is it now? The future? What month is it?

8. Record your experience.

9. What information came up? How does it nourish your life right now, or how does it call you to nourish yourself?

10. Now look at the coin you chose. How does this reading specifically inform you of the qualities of this goal and who or what might be instrumental in helping you reach it?

HEALING TOOL FOR THE
SECOND EGO CENTER

When you experience guilt or shame, your subconscious response is often to self-punish or unwittingly put yourself in situations where you are punished by others. It is your job to be your own advocate. You always have a right to protect yourself. Look at where in the past you've made excuses for toxic people, and set an intention to no longer excuse their harmful behavior.

There may also have been times when your own pain caused you to harm others. Simply being aware of these issues will heal those vestigial responses in the future. Guilt and shame are not states to remain in. They are cues to do something differently.

So write down all the things that you feel guilty or ashamed about. Read them over with an eye toward healing. Some of these things can be rectified. Some of them were life lessons that you can be careful about not repeating.

When you are done—really done—with your list, bury it, burn it, or otherwise permanently dispose of it. Make sure nothing remains on your list that you have not resolved. This is an exercise you will want to repeat regularly—even to the point of keeping a running tally of shame and blame and getting rid of them at the end of each day! For those with Second Ego Center challenges, there will always be new lists. The act of making these things conscious and putting them outside of you is a powerful patterning for the subconscious.

9

Your Third Ego Center

Flowers bloom in the desert.
And they are
The color of fire.

—Laura Day

CORRESPONDS TO: THE WILL CHAKRA
LOCATION: DIAPHRAGM/SOLAR PLEXUS

Caretakers Represent Authority

Birth	Development	Maturity
DRIVE	**COOPERATION**	**MANIFESTATION**

This Ego Center corresponds to your ability to access your drive and not have it subverted or subdued. It correlates to your ability to achieve your goals and find purpose—on your own and in collaboration with others. It relates to your ability to manifest your desires while being inclusive and included.

Properties of the Third Ego Center

Life Phase: Birth: You have the right to self-determination.

Life Phase: Development: You are tasked with the development of compromise and cooperation.

Life Phase: Maturity: You earn the ability to manifest your goals.

Ego Defense: repression, suppression

Ego Challenge: integrity

Ego Wound: powerlessness

Ego Strength: determination

Place of Joy: purpose

Polarity: drive vs. surrender

Physical Gift: vitality

Spiritual Gift: healing

Rehabilitation/Healing: living with purpose

Life Phase: **Birth**

DRIVE

Birthright: *You have the right to self-determination.*

As a physical being, you have the right to self-determination and an innate, powerful drive to that end. You are born, however, into circumstances that determine how effectively you will be able to marshal your drive and create your reality. This Ego Center's development correlates to your ability to make your way and get your way in the world.

For your Third Ego Center to be able to mature into its full power, most of the following statements needed to be true early in your development (from birth through infancy).

You were born with unbridled vitality, even if you were physically afflicted at birth; the drive to survive was fully present.

Your caretakers' attempts to succeed in life worked.

Your caretakers had a strong support system in place.

Your caretakers felt powerful.

Your caretakers were realistic. They worked toward their dreams and weren't discouraged when success didn't happen overnight.

Your caretakers were functional partners.

As an infant, your needs were met quickly and lovingly.

You were supported enough to develop pleasurable and functional connections to your caretakers and your environment.

Your impulses were supported, and you were disciplined only when appropriate. You were not shamed.

You were allowed the joy, frustration, and manageable consequences of your progress in the world as your drive led you to crawl, investigate, and reach for your desires.

Even if your family lacked resources, your caretakers were mature enough to put you first and always found appropriate ways of responding to your demands for attention and nourishment.

Your parents had the emotional stability to support all members of the family.

Your deficits were skillfully addressed, and your gifts were appropriately celebrated.

Your first efforts to exert your will, to grasp something you wanted, to master sitting, walking, toileting, and feeding yourself, were supported and applauded.

When your drive took you into dangerous territory or behaviors, your wanderings were limited by your caretakers.

Life Phase: **Development**

COOPERATION

You are tasked with the development of compromise and cooperation.

As you mature into an autonomous being, your Third Ego Center demands that you channel your drive into the ability to cooperate and compromise. When your drive productively encounters the drive of others, cooperation allows you to achieve your goals while helping others achieve theirs.

For your Third Ego Center to be able to mature into its full power, most of the following statements needed to be true in your first six or seven years of life.

As you matured, you gained an understanding of when to stand your ground and when to yield. Your caretakers set firm limits on your behavior while helping you find appropriate outlets for your frustration.

You learned how to express your desire for support and inclusion.

As you entered school, you were encouraged to follow your interests while supporting others with differing interests. You learned how to integrate yourself seamlessly into a diverse group of peers. You were able to be part of a group without losing your focus and drive as an individual.

When you failed, you were encouraged to try again, and you learned that the path to success often includes many little failures.

You mastered goal-setting and actualized your goals with discipline, patience, and determination.

Throughout your childhood, you learned the art of working with others to achieve common objectives while still making sure that your personal goals were addressed.

Modeling the standards that were set around you allowed you to subjugate unacceptable impulses and react productively to minor setbacks.

You became skilled at understanding your impulses and were able to guide them in acceptable directions.

You gained the ability to assess your role in most situations.

You valued your path, whether or not it was valued by others.

You put your well-being first and foremost.

People thought you were lucky, though in reality you were simply skilled.

You learned that if you cannot work with the world, the world will not work for or with you.

Life Phase: Maturity

MANIFESTATION

You earn the ability to manifest your goals.

During this phase, you master manifestation, where drive plus cooperation equals desired outcomes. In maturity, your drive is powerful, and your collaborative instincts are strong, allowing you to manifest easily and with support in all areas of your life.

If your Third Ego Center has been able to mature into its full power, the seeds of the following statements—along with the successful foundation work of the birth and development phases—will be true:

Your ability to cooperate channels your drive toward creating what you want.

Your drive and enthusiasm encourage others to cooperate with you.

As you reached school age, you were able to implement long-term goals.

You work elegantly with and around restrictions.

Your "luck" makes you successful in all the areas you value in your life.

Where you lead, others follow.

You easily find worthy teachers, helpers, partners, and employees who profit from collaborating with you. Your ethos is "a rising tide lifts all boats."

You are able to attract resources for any endeavor.

Failure has provided the seeds of success in every area of your life. Your life has been marked by productive second acts.

You have integrity.

Because you integrated your limitations early in life, you live with a sense of great freedom, expanding your boundaries when possible and staying within them when advisable.

You are able to change course when you find yourself on the wrong path.

Your drive affords you a clear sense of direction in your life.

Your sense of purpose has led to a sustained, dynamic engagement with life.

As you grow older, you are increasingly able to create situations where people support your vision, and your vision helps others to succeed.

As you grow older, you realize that you have achieved most of your goals, and those you haven't achieved were replaced by ones that were ultimately more meaningful.

As you near death, you will peacefully surrender to being carried home. What you manifested and shared in life has made you a vital part of the world, and your impact will continue infinitely in the relationships and structures you have manifested.

Ego Defense: Repression, Suppression

The ego defense of the Third Ego Center is an especially important one. It directs the energy of all the other Ego Centers and therefore is the center of manifestation and experience. If you struggle with your Third Ego Center, you may repress emotions and memories in order to bury your unmanageable impulses. Repression curbs destructiveness but also inhibits your drive and your ability to manifest your goals. The more mature form of suppression allows you to be aware of disturbing impulses while inhibiting them enough to function adaptively. When you repress too much, you are unable to marshal the energy and drive to create. When you suppress too little, you are impulsive, and your actions can be destructive to your life and relationships.

Ego Challenge: Integrity

The Third Ego Center is challenged by directing energy in the most economical and effective way. In the physical world, the degree to which you function with economy is the degree to which you can marshal your power. In that sense, economy is wealth. Cooperation and compromise are the essence of a well-functioning economy; when you struggle with yourself or others or circumstances, energy and resources are wasted. If the Third Ego Center is injured, you may lack the ability to work with the sometimes-conflicting elements of self, relationship, and community, and you may find yourself completely depleted even after a minor setback. You may also find that you cultivate conflict. Integrity seeks unity, the power of working "with" and not "against."

Ego Wound: Powerlessness

A wounded Third Ego Center is one that has incorporated the early experience of having your drive thwarted or, even worse, punished, leading to a sense of powerlessness. The consequence of this may be expressed through bullying, defeatism, frustration, or intolerance. Even more insidious consequences arise when the full force of one's early drive was restrained before being allowed to develop. Then the normal mechanics of finding the will and direction to move forward successfully become alien, leading to a sense of inadequacy. It can also leave you vulnerable to manipulation in situations where success could otherwise be achieved.

Ego Strength: Determination

When healthy, the Third Ego Center strength of determination allows choices to be made and reality negotiated. Setbacks are informative rather than defeating and lead to the discovery of new sources of internal power. The ability to direct and determine forward movement is the true mechanism of manifestation.

Place of Joy: Purpose

Goals are the lighthouse of the human spirit, and when your energy and direction connect to purpose, you are one with all that is useful to your life. Purpose enables you to create magic and miracles and find people with similar integrity; your shared purpose enhances your shared drive to achieve. The Third Ego Center is most vital when it cooperates with others in the creation of reality.

Polarity: Drive vs. Surrender

Drive is constructive only if you know when to tailor it for success, or, if your energy flags, when you allow yourself to be carried by others. Drive is life, while surrender is the place you safely recharge through the shared energy of spirit. The Third Ego Center longs for both absolute power to fulfill its purpose and absolute surrender in order to be carried without effort. Finding the balance between drive and surrender is the lifelong challenge of the Third Ego Center.

Physical Gift: Vitality

The Third Ego Center imparts vitality—engaged, directed life energy—to all cells, relationships, and endeavors. Your vitality overwhelms all obstacles on the way to your intended destination—and therefore you thrive. But dysfunctional forces and people can hijack your vitality to compensate for their own deficiencies; therefore, it is important to share your drive only when you choose to do so consciously. When you do, you impart life to any group or situation, and your drive manifests powerful results.

Spiritual Gift: Healing

The spiritual gift of the Third Ego Center is the ability to heal and transform the architecture of self, situation, and other through focused attention. If you have a healthy Third Ego Center, you may have noticed that throughout your life, you've been particularly adept at improving the lives of others. The same ego mechanism that gives you a powerful drive allows you to direct that drive to transform the energy around you, making you a cherished healer in your community. A strong and healthy Third Ego Center can reorganize any kind of energy into something transformative and useful.

Rehabilitation/Healing: Living with Purpose

Purpose—finding the why behind your existence—is at the core of healing the Third Ego Center. It doesn't need to be deep or existential. Raising a child, starting a company, creating art, fighting the good fight—pursuing anything that has meaning for you heals the Third Ego Center. Purpose demands that you act from a place of integrity. It keeps you on your path, albeit with an awareness that the path can change. Purpose is about making what you can out of what is, finding meaningful goals at each moment in your life, and allowing these goals—not fleeting circumstances—to provide your orientation. The key to healing the Third Ego Center is having the perseverance to move your purpose forward. It can also, incidentally, help you live longer.

Injured Development of the Third Ego Center

Answer the questions that follow honestly to understand what might have interfered with the healthy use and development of your Third Ego Center. At the end of this chapter, you will find an exercise to help heal injured Third Ego Centers.

1. Did you have to repress natural impulses prematurely?

2. Did your family insist on "premature" autonomy—being independent before you were ready?

3. Were mistakes harshly punished, making you tentative about your competence and sense of direction in the world?

4. Did inadequate rules and consequences leave you ill-equipped to excel within real-world constraints?

5. Were you never taught how to cooperate and compromise?

6. Did your family have overly rigid, inconsistent, or absent boundaries?

7. Did your family circumstances exclude you from participating in a larger community?

8. Were you born into a family where autonomy was undermined?

9. Did your parents overprotect you, keeping you from learning experiences?

10. Were you given the sense that you could do no wrong? Did this delusion prevent you from learning social norms?

11. Were you a member of a social or economic group where you had few opportunities to follow your own interests and desires because of prejudice, poverty, or a social dictate against individuality?

12. Did you lack caring, firm, and reliable teachers and leaders?

13. Did your immature impulses lead you into dangerous territory?

14. Did *no* mean *maybe* in your house?

15. Were your efforts never good enough? Were your talents undervalued?

16. Were you shamed for your immaturity, even though your behavior was age-appropriate?

17. Were the people in positions of authority unstable, leaving you unable to trust?

18. Were you abused at the hands of those in authority?

Signs of an Afflicted Third Ego Center

If you answered yes to any of the above "Injured Development" questions about your childhood, you may experience the following challenges in your adult life:

You lack faith in your own abilities. You continually second-guess yourself.

When you have an idea or intuition that could change your life, you are unable to find support.

You lack direction.

You attract people who rely on your drive but fail to bring their own energy to achieve mutual goals.

You attract parasitic people who take advantage of your strength and abilities.

You are unable to differentiate between trustworthy and untrustworthy leaders, endeavors, and situations.

You don't understand the difference between getting your way and true satisfaction.

You are overly acquiescent and compliant.

If you weren't given sufficient boundaries and were an overly willful child, you struggle with perceiving or accepting the natural hierarchies of life.

You find yourself constantly disappointed with others' lack of support for your ideas and endeavors.

You often get into trouble with teachers, employers, or the law because you do things your way without a clear sense of consequences.

You are unable to cooperate with societal expectations such as monogamy or deadlines.

You lack the discipline to organize and complete projects.

You are a jack of all trades and a master of none as you follow every whim without the will to see things through.

You are belligerent or egotistical and often make enemies.

You lack the trust to accept help.

You do the same dysfunctional thing over and over, expecting a different result.

You bully when things don't go your way.

You find it hard to learn from others or change the way you do things.

You are easily manipulated by others.

The Results of a Misdirected Third Ego Center

- digestive issues

- respiratory issues

- bad luck

- codependency

- lack of support from others

- the inability to accurately assess your skills, resulting in crushing failures

- alienating and toxic behaviors that push others away

- an inability to direct enough power and drive to achieve your goals

- a sense of purposelessness

- seeking adrenaline in unhealthy ways

- being frequently used and manipulated by others

- an inability to create anything of sustaining value

- OCD, anxiety, depression, oppositional behaviors, and rage

How to Heal the Third Ego Center

- Adhere to appropriate codes of conduct.

- Be flexible whenever you can.

- Engage in productive, community-oriented tasks that bring pleasure and joy.

- Find and follow your passion with commitment.

- Identify goals.

- Find appropriate ways to experience safely the full power of your energy and drive, such as movement, voicing, writing, art, or any unbridled *private* expression of your force.

- Check that feelings, actions, and goals reflect your true desires.

- Say no when you need to.

- Challenge your limits.

- Address issues of codependency; foster independence.

- Relinquish control.

- Apologize.

- Avoid people, habits, and situations that sap/limit/inhibit your vitality.

- Rely on determination instead of faith.

Healing Questions

It is helpful to write down your responses to these questions and update them as you do the work in this book.

1. Am I being controlled by others' demands, values, or expectations?

2. Do I need to control others in order to feel safe?

3. Do I allow myself to be guided by others?

4. Am I a valuable member of a helpful, supportive community?

5. Do I live by my values?

6. Do I persevere until I meet my goals?

7. Can I cooperate or change direction when it's the most effective thing to do?

8. Can I say no and mean it?

9. Can people count on me when I give my word?

10. Can I tolerate frustration?

11. Can I accept what I cannot control?

12. Do I have a place where I belong—in my home, my relationships, my community? A place where I can safely surrender to others?

13. When I pray, do I feel heard?

14. Do I not have access to the full extent of my energy and enthusiasm because I hold myself back?

When You Heal Your Third Ego Center

* You are a master manifester.

* You attract helpful people and authentic partners.

* You live your purpose unapologetically while encouraging the purpose of others.

* You know why you're alive and you live well.

- Wherever you are, things/people/events organize around you.

- You place your trust in reliable people.

- You accurately evaluate situations and prospects.

- You feel peaceful.

- You accept reality without being defeated by it.

- You do not engage in losing ventures.

- You respond in the moment to what is before you, without hypervigilant control.

- You are resilient.

- You find support in every situation.

- When you are ready, the teacher, investor, or lover appears.

- You have willpower. You can manage ambition for a desired result.

- You live the Serenity Prayer: "God grant me the serenity to accept the things I cannot change, the courage to change the things I can, and the wisdom to know the difference."

Daily Assertions

I choose.

"No" is a complete sentence.

When the student is ready, the teacher appears.

No matter where I start, I end up where I choose.

Working with reality creates my destiny.

Integrity is my North Star.

Feeling good is not the same as doing good.

I am the master of my own impulses.

The obstacles are the path.

When I create a path for others, I clear a new path for myself.

I can go with the flow.

Controlling others saps my energy. Is this a sacrifice I want to make?

Every time I control/redirect my impulses, I become a master manifester.

Compromise is not a sacrifice.

I choose where to engage and with whom. I can always revise that choice.

Mistakes are part of success.

Effort is a healing exercise in and of itself.

Insight gives me what I want or it changes my desires into ones that serve me.

When I commit, I show up.

INTUITIVE TOOL FOR THE
THIRD EGO CENTER

Pause whatever you're doing and pick a coin. Don't look at it. Take a deep breath and allow that breath to make the totality of your being available. Expand your awareness with your breath as you experience conscious access to the powerful wholeness of you. The treasures in you that have been suppressed, old bits of self and experience, become available. The fragments of self that live below your conscious experience reveal themselves and remain in your attention long enough to direct you to the next perception. Latent bits of hopes, fears, and memories now have the energy to reemerge and be understood and released into a healed version of you, bringing with them the tools you need to re-create your life.

You may not be consciously aware of this process, but it is happening nevertheless and will reveal itself to you in the synchronicities that follow in your everyday life, now changed by the power of your awareness.

You are joining your ego—your individuality—to spirit, to the one, infinite energy of which you are a part. You are not surrendering the ego. The self you inhabit is the contact boundary between pure energy and its expression as you. As an individual connecting with the source, your awareness directs your impact on the world, giving you the power to change both yourself and the world around you. You have access to all knowledge, power, and wisdom—all of reality—as you nourish spirit and self as both separate and one. This is the act of constructive, active mindfulness. Take a moment to recognize this being of true self you have encountered.

Now let's do a focused healing that directs the power of your presence and intention toward creating change in the physical world.

Take a long, deep breath and bring your attention, your breath, and both hands to the Third Ego Center: the solar plexus. Allow that area of your body—your being—to become your focus. Each subsequent breath you take gains power and easily displaces old patterns, feelings, and habits that no longer serve you. You direct, you detail, you manifest your healing.

As you do this, you will notice that your experience of yourself is changing because your physical, electrical, and emotional structures are changing. What you thought you wanted when you began this healing has transformed. You now manifest the truest expression of those desires, not from injury or lack but from the most integral knowledge of your own power. Now consciously connected to everything around you, you choose your own place in the structure of reality.

Bring your attention to your hands. You may find that while one of them remains at your solar plexus, the other feels drawn to a different Ego Center. It may even move from one Ego Center to another and then to another. Give yourself the time and freedom for this process to play out until you experience all the parts of you, organized and aligned—where they need to be to make up the powerful organism you are. You may notice that at different moments, you meet resistance. The experience of healing may slow or even stop. Responsively, with powerful and intuitive direction but without force, allow your breath and intention to collaborate with the energy to find a way to create your healing. You may have to do this many times as you heal your body, your experience, your life, and your being.

Now, extend your balanced, healed, directed energy into the world around you using the power of your breath and the Third Ego Center. Notice that with every breath, your intentions become clearer. As you direct your will from a healthy place, you direct the world. When you encounter a will or a pattern of events that is as healthy, clear, and strong as your own, you will recognize each other and cooperate to make what each of you are creating even stronger. As your healed ambition reorganizes your world, you will find that, seemingly out of the blue, the support you need comes to you, and the opportunity to support others in healthy ways appears as well. When you learn as you teach, support as you are supported, love as you are loved, and self-heal as you heal others, you easily create what you envision and are part of the success of others' creations.

As your life is directed by the healthiest part of you, become aware of something or someone you would like to heal. It may be a person, a corporation, a relationship, a country, a world. Your breath begins to heal the object of your attention the same way it is healing you. This is the gift of the Third Ego Center and your gift of healing to the world.

As you put this energetic structure into practice, you will find that you can apply it to everything in your life in a matter of seconds. Your intentional restructuring of reality becomes a simple part of how you function.

> You are the healer.
> When you heal yourself, you heal the world.
> When you heal the world, you heal yourself.

Now look at the number on your coin.

What you just experienced was the healing key to that goal. Notice what occurs in the coming days and weeks as the healing takes effect. Notice how the information you received illuminated the areas where healing made an impact. You are the healer.

HEALING TOOL FOR THE
THIRD EGO CENTER

In equal counts: take a breath, hold the breath, and release the breath. Start with four: inhale for four counts, hold for four counts, release for four counts. You will find that, over time, you can do this for longer counts.

Your diaphragm is the physical seat of your impulses. It is where consciousness meets the subconscious and where intention is propelled into the environment. When you inhale, you take in the energy you need. When you hold the breath, you integrate that energy in a productive way, signaling to your brain that you are safe and in control. When you exhale, you put the energy you have now reorganized back into the environment.

This is both a powerful physiological/psychological exercise and a powerful spiritual exercise. You organize and direct the unified drive of self and spirit in a constructive way while making energetic contact with the world. After a while, this simple exercise will organize your every breath around creating your best life. It's a wonderful exercise to do when working out. You pattern yourself to direct your natural vitality with every breath!

You may also notice that, as you practice this exercise, internal obstacles arise in the form of a memory, a reaction, an awareness, a feeling. You may even attract obstacles in the world around you that prompt you to organize your energy appropriately for change. Allow all of these to be teachers. Stay determined in your goal and you will see results. Effortlessness is a myth. The power of your Third Ego Center comes alive with intentionally directed effort. This is the healing gift of the Third Ego Center.

10

Your Fourth Ego Center

For each, in his own way, finds what it is he must love,
and loves it; the window becomes a mirror; whatever
it is that we love, that is who we are.

—DAVID LEAVITT, *The Lost Language of Cranes*

CORRESPONDS TO: THE HEART CHAKRA
LOCATION: HEART

Caretakers Represent Love and Worth

Birth	Development	Maturity
LOVE	WORTH	DIGNITY

The Fourth Ego Center corresponds with the degree to which others assign value to you and the opportunities, remuneration, adoration, and honors they bestow on you. It correlates to your ability to be of worth and feel of worth to situations, people, and yourself. It structures your ability to connect with resources, find things/people/experiences of value, and experience contentment.

Properties of the Fourth Ego Center

Life Phase: Birth: You have the right to be valued.

Life Phase: Development: You are tasked with being useful.

Life Phase: Maturity: You earn dignity.

Ego Defense: sublimation, projection

Ego Challenge: self-esteem

Ego Wound: worthlessness/emptiness

Ego Strength: grace

Place of Joy: connection

Polarity: merging vs. individuation

Physical Gift: beauty

Spiritual Gift: telepathy

Rehabilitation/Healing: forgiveness/discernment

Life Phase: **Birth**

LOVE

Birthright: *You have the right to be valued.*

Your fourth right as a physical being is your right to be loved and treasured simply because you exist. Long before self-worth becomes a developmental task, you are born into a set of circumstances that determine how much you will value yourself and how well you will attract value to you.

For your Fourth Ego Center to be able to mature into its full power, the seeds of most of the following statements needed to be true early in your development (from birth through infancy).

When you were born, your caretakers loved and respected each other and felt valued in the world.

Your caretakers felt they could connect deeply and authentically with others.

You felt treasured from the moment you were born. You were lovingly held, and the seeds of self-acceptance and self-respect were implanted in you.

Even as an infant, you felt not only that you had value but that you delighted those around you when you choose to do so—and you were delighted by them.

Your caretakers had a deep attachment to you, to others, and to what they considered valuable in life. Those attachments formed the healthy emotional matrix of your world.

Even if you suffered the early loss of one of your attachments, caring, engaged adults made your emotional transition healthy. You were supported in appropriately mourning lost attachments and given the tools to form new ones.

If other children were born after you, you felt your value as an elder sibling. You had the awareness that your role could change without being diminished.

Life Phase: **Development**

WORTH

You are tasked with being useful.

As you matured, the Fourth Ego Center experienced the importance of adding value to situations and acknowledging the value of others. The experience of being treasured by your caretakers made you know your value in situations where you might otherwise have been exploited.

For your Fourth Ego Center to be able to develop into its full power, the seeds of most of the following statements needed to be true in your first six or seven years of life:

You were guided in adding value to situations, relationships, and projects.

As you gained more exposure to the world, your sense of your value may have been challenged by bigotry, bullying, or being on a lower rung of your academic, athletic, or social group. A foundation of self-worth and the embrace of authentic values carried you through those times and helped you find a successful identity that was uniquely yours.

Even though a high value was placed on kindness and moral behavior, you were loved for who you were and not for what you did. When things went wrong, your value as a human being was never placed in question, and you felt empowered to change behaviors that did not reflect your values.

As you matured, you mastered your emotional triggers and gained the tools to metabolize stress instead of displacing it onto your environment. With your growing self-worth, you were able to sublimate the challenges of life, transforming your destructive impulses and experiences into creations of beauty and worth.

Your juvenile ego defense of displacement—the transference of a difficult feeling from self to another (e.g., you are frustrated by not being invited to sit with the popular kids at lunch, so you blow up at what your caretaker prepared for dinner)—was directed toward self-awareness, so that you were able to identify sources of upset and felt resourceful enough to deal with them.

Your "evolved" Fourth Ego Center defense of sublimation added to your uniqueness by redirecting destructive drives and impulses, along with life's disappointments, into socially acceptable situations, relationships, and goals, and also into products of beauty and worth, enhancing your life and the lives of those around you.

In mastering sublimation, you were able to safely make more of your inner conflicts and drives as fuel for success.

Your positive early experiences structured enough of a self to allow you to deeply attach to others and experience their deep attachment to you without being engulfed.

You learned that you and others were free to exist as separate yet connected beings.

You were able to create and nurture what you valued, whether it was a relationship, a position of standing among your peers, a skill set, or material security.

Friendships and relationships were mutually satisfying. You instinctively avoided destructive people.

In relationships, you were able to maintain a balance between loving the other person and valuing yourself. In situations that required some sacrifice, you had internal reserves and external support to endure them without injury.

In those inevitable times when your friendships or relationships ended, you were able to grieve, find support, and move on.

Your adulthood was supported by enduring friendships.

Your strong values helped you create and attract beauty.

Life Phase: **Maturity**

DIGNITY

You earn an esteemed place in the world.

As your innate sense of your own value joined with your ability to develop things of value with others, you lived in the reflection of your own best self. Life, love, success, and all that you value are drawn to your dignity, and you impart it to everything and everyone around you.

If your Fourth Ego Center has been able to mature into its full power, the seeds of the following statements, along with the successful foundation work of the birth and development phases, will be true:

As you matured, your abilities were valued and rewarded.

You were accomplished enough to feel treasured. Your natural self effortlessly attracted respect and dignity.

Your relationships were mutually beneficial. Even when they ended, you were able to move on, always learning from your experiences.

Your wealth was available to be enjoyed and shared.

Although your past wasn't perfect, you have been able to look back with compassion, not bitterness.

As you aged, you were able to experience the gifts of maturity without becoming fixated on the loss of youth. Each stage brought with it a new beauty, value, and power.

Your community grew into a resource for support, purpose, and connection.

You lent your power and beauty to the next generation and to ideas and projects that made the world a better place.

You parented generously, imparting values and discernment through kindness. Your children were guided and nourished by their reflection in your love.

Younger people adored you and showered you with their idealistic love. You were at ease with your ability to attract love, support, and resources, which made your later years full of love, companionship, and ease.

Those who died as you got older helped you prepare for your own fearless death. You will meet your death with an experience of the loving arms that supported you throughout your life and will guide your transition to the next phase. You leave those you loved well-equipped to live on without you.

Ego Defense: Sublimation, Projection

When, as a child, you were unable to tolerate the frustration of being undervalued, you may have displaced that frustration onto other people and other things. For example, you may have been angry because you were rejected by a classmate, but, unable to express that anger directly, you went home and erupted at family members over a minor issue. As your ego strength grows, you acquire the ability to sublimate, to create something of value from the pain of your unmet needs and maladaptive impulses.

Ego Challenge: Self-Esteem

If you were valued and then taught to develop your self-worth, then self-love and self-esteem are inherent parts of your structure and remain there in the face of challenges. With an afflicted or challenged Fourth Ego Center, you may find it hard to maintain self-worth in the face of difficulties. It may be a struggle to heal what you recognize as your own toxic qualities. You may attract devaluing experiences in an effort to heal this wound.

Ego Wound: Worthlessness/Emptiness

An injured Fourth Ego Center cannot experience its own worth unless it gets positive feedback from the environment. And if truly damaged, it has trouble feeling worth even when clearly loved and valued. A damaged Fourth Ego Center makes you feel empty whenever you are alone, as the company of self has little value. This makes it difficult to maintain self-worth when you are *not* alone—for instance, in relationships. It makes you feel undervalued and under-rewarded by others, and it can lead to a lack of self-care.

We are born prizing our caretakers above all else, and the reflection that comes back to us from them is what gives us our first sense of self. As we mature, we extend that love to our home, our community, our values, and our relationships. Inevitably, though, we are betrayed by some of those things. When that happens, what we once connected to from our core suddenly feels worthless or even harmful. Because connection is an essential part of the fabric of self, our very sense of self-worth is torn. Rejection/betrayal is the death of something we invested in; mourning is its companion. However, these disappointments bear a silver lining: they can lead to discovering true worth in yourself and in your environment, even when others are not affirming it.

Ego Strength: Grace

When the Fourth Ego Center is in balance, it imparts ease and beauty in even the most difficult situations. Where other Ego Centers drive, express, and/or assert, the Fourth Ego Center charms. As it strengthens, you will find grace emerging to work with—not against—the energy you use in creating what you want. You are able to make the mundane lovely and experience loveliness in the mundane.

Place of Joy: Connection

As your heart beats, it sends out an electrical signal—a call—to the world. The heart wishes to connect. Indeed, the place of joy for the Fourth Ego Center is connection—the world's response to the call of the heart. In connection with people, ideas, and even places, each element is dignified and elevated. It is the essence of the greeting *namaste*: "The divine in me bows to the divine in you."

Polarity: Merging vs. Individuation

Balance requires that we experience "center," which is located at that place in the heart where we connect simultaneously to ourselves and to what is around us. The ongoing challenge of the Fourth Ego Center is to balance the desire to surrender completely to the flow of spirit—oneness, anonymity—with the exquisite excitement of being alive.

Being an individual with an ego is hard work. It requires that we constantly redefine self in response to the changes going on around us. But the reward for that is our ability to create: to live in the material world, contribute to it, and share in what is most precious about it.

And spirit cannot create; only ego can. Safeguarding both ego and spirit, weighing the needs of the self against the needs of the collective/other, and interacting without merging and losing oneself—this is the task of the Fourth Ego Center.

Physical Gift: Beauty

The physical gift of the Fourth Ego Center is the ability to find, express, and embody beauty in all aspects of life. Healthy Fourth Ego Center people are seen as beautiful irrespective of conventional standards of beauty. They cherish their own unique beauty and see past false images and values. They invest in—and effortlessly attract—only those things, people, and situations that are of real worth.

Innately understanding your own beauty and self-worth positions you in your life in a new and transformative way. It demands that you attach profoundly, mourn loss, learn from betrayal without cutting yourself off from experience, and clear the way for the next abundant gifts life has to offer you.

Spiritual Gift: Telepathy

The heart is not only the physical home of love and compassion; it also has the telepathic ability to send and receive information over long distances. Telepathy is the spiritual gift of the Fourth Ego Center. As you have read in earlier chapters, this ability has been well researched, with studies as far back as the 1950s showing that telepathy is actively present in our lives. You are in nonlocal communication with others all the time, and all of us have had some experience of this. Most of the conversations you have in your head are actually "heard" by others, albeit often without their conscious awareness of it. Others are reacting to you just as you are reacting to them, sometimes without knowing exactly why. Whom you engage with telepathically and how you engage with them are the most powerful determinants of how well you function in your life and how others perceive and respond to you.

Rehabilitation/Healing: Forgiveness/Discernment

We are hardwired to hold on to adverse experiences. However, to make full use of your Fourth Ego Center, you cannot allow an emotional or psychological injury to occupy your energy and attention for an extended period of time. Forgiveness creates a filter of discernment that disengages you from the harm, frees up space for you to connect with what you value, and allows you to recognize and avoid future threats.

We forgive not because it's more "spiritual" to do so but because forgiveness reclaims the parts of our self that are wastefully engaged with the experience of harm. Forgiveness is especially difficult in ongoing relationships. It is the sophisticated skill of the Fourth Ego Center to discern which dynamics are acceptable, which are unacceptable, and which call for forgiveness.

Injured Development of the Fourth Ego Center

Answer the questions that follow honestly to understand what might have interfered with the healthy use and development of your Fourth Ego Center. At the end of this chapter, you will find an exercise to help heal injured Fourth Ego Centers.

1. Were you born into a family where attachment carried inappropriate burdens?

2. Did you feel you could lose the love of your caretakers by not being enough or by being too much?

3. Were your caretakers emotionally unavailable?

4. Were your caretakers so needy that you often had to choose between love of self and love of other?

5. Were the objects of your love violent, critical, or inconsistent?

6. Was the love you received conditional upon your being, appearing, or behaving in a certain way?

7. Did you lose a caretaker at an early age without adequate replacement?

8. Were you the least favored child?

9. Was there so much tension at home that you had trouble connecting with peers at school?

10. Were you made to feel guilty about your emotional needs?

11. Did you have to disconnect from your need for love, approval, and support in order to survive?

12. Were your efforts given little or no recognition of importance?

13. Were you indulged without having to be of value to others in your life?

14. Were you overly criticized?

15. Did your caretakers only value you for your part in their drama?

16. Did you treasure people or ideas that betrayed you?

Signs of an Afflicted Fourth Ego Center

If you answered yes to any of the above "Injured Development" questions about your childhood, you may experience the following challenges in your adult life:

You have a hard time attracting love, partnership, friendship, and relationships, or you attract unkind people who undervalue you.

You undervalue others, especially when the newness of the relationship is gone.

You are afraid to open up to other people.

You overreact to the usual imperfections in love and life, seeing them as a reflection of your worth.

You are hypercritical and have perfectionistic standards about your appearance, your work, your home, your family, and your friends.

You are vulnerable to criticism from others.

You underrate yourself or overcompensate by being pretentious.

You have financial problems while being underrecognized or underpaid at work.

You cling to unsatisfying relationships and blame yourself for other people's inability to love.

You adopt the standards and ethics of others even when they don't suit you.

You are terrified of abandonment and/or losing the things you treasure. You dread aging and feel you will no longer be wanted.

You have trouble being content even under the best of circumstances.

You value things that are actually worthless.

The Results of a Misdirected Fourth Ego Center

- chronic grief

- chronic sense of emptiness

- depression

- inability to form healthy, enduring relationships

- heart and lung problems

- inability to sustain worthwhile situations

- inability to generate or hold on to wealth

- greed

- an unenchanted life—no fun!

- feeling unloved

- inability to attract an adequate mate, job, home, or life situation

- a lack of gratitude or a lack of things to be grateful for

- having less than others in your community in any area of life

- being perceived by others as not beautiful or valuable

- loneliness

How to Heal the Fourth Ego Center

- Engaging in mutually supportive contact in all areas of life.

- Connecting regularly with a loving community that values you or, if you don't have one, showing up in groups you want to be a part of. Practicing apology and forgiveness as a life skill.

- Nurturing friendships that are reciprocal and intimate.

- Recognizing your value by using it in service to others.

- Being authentic with yourself and others.

- Finding ways to connect with yourself that are supportive and constructive.

- Embracing soothing and healing practices, such as breath-work, walking, praying.

- Redirecting unacceptable drives or challenging experiences through creative expression.

- Expressing gratitude through service and generosity to others.

- Finding the beauty in all things and creating beauty when possible.

- Immersing in beauty—in nature, at museums, at concerts, or on a playground with laughing children.

- Allowing imperfect beings to love you imperfectly.

- Bringing grace and beauty into everything you do, adding enchantment, ritual, adornment, magic, art, and self-care into your daily practices.

Healing Questions

It is helpful to write down your responses to these questions and update them as you do the work in this book.

1. Did I connect with others today in an authentic way?

2. Did I find beauty today?

3. Did I share something with the world today?

4. Did I allow myself to perceive something precious today, whether an experience, an idea, an interaction, or a feeling?

5. Did I forgive myself and others today?

6. Did I nurture my work today?

7. Have I done something of service for others today?

8. Have I allowed others to serve me today?

9. Did I value people and affirm their value today?

10. Did I get enough affirmation of my own value today?

11. Am I loving and forgiving myself today?

12. Did I do something to add value to my life today?

13. Did I forgive a betrayal today, taking the lessons with me and leaving the injury behind?

When You Heal Your Fourth Ego Center

- You will find that *what you do* and *who you are* are appreciated and rewarded.

- You will be partnered with good people in everything you do.

- Your relationships, even the challenging ones, will change for the better or fall away.

- The first sign of your healing work may be a raise, a new job, finding true love, or a transformation in an existing relationship.

- You may discover that your beloved hobby can make you money or that people you meet are willing to support your dreams.

- You will find new strength and attractiveness at every age, while some of the goals of your youth are realized with even greater passion and depth.

- You will find new contentment in the people and things in your life, and new sources of contentment may enter the picture.

- You will spend less time holding on and holding things in and more time celebrating reality.

- Life will enchant you, even at its most mundane.

- You will attract wealth easily in all areas of your life.

- You will learn how to use betrayals to identify people, things, and situations of true merit.

Daily Assertions

I am worthy.

I don't need to be perfect to be lovable.

I don't need to be valued to have value.

When I value myself, I bring value to others.

When I am not loved, I am not in the right place.

I forgive myself for loving myself imperfectly.

Love exists for me. I love and accept myself.

I am a work in progress, and I am loving myself and accepting myself more every day.

My love is a valuable resource that I share as a precious gift.

What I have belongs to no one but me. I choose whom to share it with.

Although people are imperfect, I embody the perfection of love, and I work on its expression every day.

Even when I feel alone, I am deeply and powerfully connected to the world around me. I can choose to live that connection in my daily life. In short, I am not alone.

I have compassion for the person I was, and I admire the person I am becoming.

I forgive others, because I choose to attach only to what is life-affirming and life-sustaining.

I forgive myself. If I can't fix it, I forget it.

I accept valid criticism and use it to build a stronger self.

What I value exists for me. My sacred path is to find it.

Dignity cannot be taken from me.

I am an alchemist; it is my destiny to make the mundane precious.

INTUITIVE TOOL FOR THE FOURTH EGO CENTER

Everyone experiences negative thought loops now and then. These loops can contain memories of people who do not benefit you, even if you don't know them, like an angry driver who cut you off or someone who was rude to you in a check-out line. Whatever initiated the event doesn't matter. You are responsible for deciding whether or not these inner conversations should continue. You also have the power to change their tone.

Bring to mind one such incident or person that provokes negative, obsessive thought. With a pen and paper, take some notes on how you might shift that conversation in a way that is empowering, comforting, and productive. Try multiple approaches. You will soon notice a difference. Challenge yourself to maintain this new tone in the future.

The skills you are cultivating with this intuitive tool will also help you maintain meaningful connections with those who have died. When we think about communicating with the dead, we often assume they will express clichéd sentiments, such as that they forgive you or that they are in a better place. But this is not always the case. Your deceased sister may just as easily scold you for staining her favorite sweater! You can make demands and hear theirs. You can decline to engage or fulfill a request. When you release expectations, you allow real communication to occur. (This also works with the living!)

Telepathy should have a goal, even if that goal is only to share closeness and connection, because telepathy without a goal creates clutter that takes attention away from your engagement with life. So write down whom you want to communicate with and the goal for your interaction. Don't worry if your goals change at any point; just placing them outside of your messy mind will enable you to process what you need to do to create better communication.

You may also want to make a list of people you no longer want to communicate with. Be aware that when you cut someone off telepathically, they will often call you or try to make contact in another way. This is also evidence of the existence of telepathy—and its power. I often tell people who obsess about someone not calling, "Why would the person call? You are already overwhelming them with communications!"

The way to redirect telepathy away from destructive conversations is to have a short list of people you *want* to communicate with, what you want to communicate, and your goal in the communication (which may change as you listen). You may, at first, have to redirect many times a day or even every hour, but over time, you will master the skill of keeping your field clear!

Be as good a telepathic listener as you are a sender. Ideally, telepathy should be a dialogue with opportunities for growth on both sides. And remember: what you say to yourself about yourself is "heard" by all. Be truthful, as telepathy immediately knows a lie, but be kind.

Here is a short list of ways to clean up telepathy. Put these suggestions into practice and you will be amazed at how quickly your life changes!

1. Ask yourself: "What telepathic conversations am I having that are useless, unrewarding, or hurtful?"

2. Consider whether you want to change the way you are communicating with someone or whether you simply want to cut off the communication.

3. If you want to change the communication, listen closely and try to respond in a new way. It will take repetition and practice not to engage in an old paradigm.

4. Ask yourself: "What or who do *I* want to connect with in my world? What do I want the result to be?"

5. Pay close attention to finding the senses, imagery, and feelings that will get the results you want. Experience those in a way that is real and truthful as you connect with another. You will always be shifting as the conversation evolves.

6. When your conversations wander to unhelpful places and people, shift to a desired conversation. Again, this takes practice and repetition.

7. Notice when what you are "saying" isn't truthful, because it will not be "heard" as truth by someone else. Try to reframe that "truth" in a way that serves you, and then acknowledge and process the lies you may be telling yourself.

HEALING TOOLS FOR THE FOURTH EGO CENTER

Sit or stand in front of a mirror. Look at yourself without merging but as the person you love the most. What do you vow to do for yourself? Say it aloud: "What do I vow to do for myself?" If you cannot conjure a feeling of love for yourself, see in your reflection someone you love beyond measure. Touch that image with your love, and, as you do, allow the image to become you.

Another powerful tool for healing the Fourth Ego Center is "well-wishing," or blessing. In every interaction, find the place in you that genuinely wishes others well. It doesn't have to be from a place of attachment (though sometimes it is). Rather, have it come from the part of you that values kindness, beauty, and integrity. Notice how all of your relationships and the impact you have on situations change through that single, simple act. You will find that this tool also helps you filter out experiences and people that are not a blessing to you.

11

Your Fifth Ego Center

If you hear a voice within you say, "You cannot paint,"
then by all means paint, and that voice will be silenced.

—Vincent van Gogh

CORRESPONDS TO: THE THROAT CHAKRA
LOCATION: THROAT

Caretakers Represent Truth and
Authentic Expression

Birth	Development	Maturity
VOICE	CONVERSATION	LEADERSHIP

Your Fifth Ego Center corresponds to your ability to communicate, to "be heard" in the world, to find helpful mentors, and to lead effectively. It controls your capacity for recognizing, accepting, and working with truth, so that your engagement with the world creates opportunities to lead yourself and others to a more desired reality. It relates to your experience of authentic and secure expression and the ability to identify and evaluate other people's integrity.

Properties of the Fifth Ego Center

Life Phase: Birth: You have the right to be heard.

Life Phase: Development: You are tasked with the development of conversation.

Life Phase: Maturity: You earn the gift of leadership.

Ego Defense: denial

Ego Challenge: equanimity

Ego Wound: pretense

Ego Strength: accuracy/acuity

Place of Joy: harmony

Polarity: evidence vs. belief

Physical Gift: persuasion

Spiritual Gift: clairaudience

Rehabilitation/Healing: truth

Life Phase: **Birth**

VOICE

Birthright: *You have the right to be heard.*

Your fifth right as a physical being is to have a voice—to affirm your existence and your experience and to be heard and elicit a response. Long before you have conscious communication, you are born into circumstances that determine how much access you will have to your own true voice, how you will use that voice, how the world will respond to your demands, and how you, in turn, will perceive that response as a reflection of your truth.

For your Fifth Ego Center to be able to mature into its full power, the seeds of most of the following statements needed to be true early in your development (from birth through infancy).

When you were born, your caretakers communicated well with each other and their community.

Your caretakers had a functional grasp of reality.

Your caretakers lived with both conviction and equanimity.

Your caretakers modeled a flexibility of expression and presented their ideas in a way that was productive and accepted.

Your caretakers responded appropriately when you expressed your needs.

Your caretakers' communications were honest and age-appropriate guides to adaptive behavior.

You received reliable guidance from secondary caretakers, such as grandparents, babysitters, and teachers.

You learned to adapt your expression to different situations and caretakers without having to compromise your needs.

You enjoyed the sound of your own voice and felt empowered to use it to express yourself and get your needs met.

Life Phase: **Development**

CONVERSATION

You are tasked with the development of conversation.

As you matured, your voice joined the voices of others, developing the many sophisticated layers needed to be heard by your ever-expanding world. You were able to hear and respond to others in a way that supported your goals while affirming theirs. Reciprocal challenges and affirmations—conversation—gave you context for all the elements of self and your place in the world.

For your Fifth Ego Center to be able to mature into its full power, the seeds of most of the following statements needed to be true in your first six or seven years of life.

As you mastered language, you learned to use it skillfully, flexibly, and appropriately to express yourself and elicit a positive response from others.

You were supported in giving voice to even your most difficult feelings.

You learned that being heard and getting your way were not synonymous, and you learned to adapt your expectations and moderate your expression.

You learned early on that there are many voices in a family and community, and you were supported in reconciling the truths of others with your own growing integrity.

When there were conflicting messages, you found trustworthy guidance within yourself.

You were able to hear which voices and messages in your environment could not be trusted and which ones were in harmony with your own truth.

You skillfully used your voice to set boundaries, build intimacy, share ideas, gain support, defend, express, protest, attract, and inspire.

If you had siblings, everyone had a voice, and conversation led to the pleasure of harmony.

As your own voice matured, you were able to integrate different styles of communication into your repertoire, which broadened your opportunities in the world.

You felt heard by your caretakers even when what you voiced was not always met with agreement or the desired result.

Those inevitable moments when you felt unheard by the wider world did not destroy your faith in your ability to communicate. Instead, you found new ways to be heard and removed yourself from situations where the integrity of your expression was compromised.

You employed denial, the Fifth Ego Center defense, to ensure that information you were not ready to see remained unseen until your ego had developed the tools to address it.

You learned an inner language of self-encouragement to meet challenging situations.

Your perceptions were based on truth. There were no burdensome family secrets to protect.

You attracted reliable teachers when you needed guidance or a new skill.

You were able to recognize what was real and what wasn't and act accordingly.

You gathered evidence about what would constitute appropriate action, but it didn't crush your beliefs, which continued to inspire you to expand your reach.

Life Phase: **Maturity**

LEADERSHIP

You earn the gift of leadership.

In maturity, if you have a healthy Fifth Ego Center, your voice is clear and you have learned to conduct dialogues appropriately, giving you many lucid ways in which to express your integrity and leadership so that others can hear and be inspired. Your ability to collaborate has given you teachers to rely upon and has led you to a world that reflects your clearest voice back to you. People join you in your endeavors with enthusiasm and appreciation.

If your Fifth Ego Center has been able to mature into its full power, the seeds of most of the following statements, along with the successful foundation work of the birth and development phases, will be true:

As you matured into a successful and respected person, you were able to integrate difficult truths about yourself, others, and the world, and this mastery diminished the need for denial as a Fifth Ego Center defense.

You had an empowering life narrative that resonated positively with others. Your story was flexible enough to shift when you gained new understanding.

Through dialogue with others, the world opened up to you. As you gained expertise and confidence, your voice became a guide for others—interpersonally and professionally.

When you wanted to create change in your life, your reliable and convincing voice attracted an enthusiastic response from the world around you.

When you chose to take the lead, people followed you, to the benefit of all.

You sought harmony in every situation and conversation, and when harmony proved impossible, you removed yourself from the dialogue.

Your ability to bear honest witness was a valued gift you gave to others.

Your equanimity told you when it was best to lead, follow, or find another way.

You allowed others to bear witness for you and, when needed, to be the keepers and reminders of your own clear voice.

The conversations that you had with loved ones continued after their death. You both spoke and listened as you continued to create mutually supportive interactions.

As the end of your life nears, your experience of being heard and being able to listen to others will allow you to prepare for the transition into death. Your ability to inspire a harmony of voices in life has supported your experience of your own unique self as a treasured part of the unified vibration of spirit.

Ego Defense: Denial

When reality is so overwhelming as to threaten your functioning, your subconscious silences the threat with the Fifth Ego defense of denial. You pick and choose what to experience instead of taking in all that is there. As you mature, this defense grows less necessary. You become able to suppress distress without denying truth, so that you can function in the world while maintaining enough awareness of reality to respond effectively.

Ego Challenge: Equanimity

Other people's points of view can be disturbing. They can challenge your sense of well-being and expose contradictions. Although your interpretation of reality is what guides you, you also need to have a respect for the right of others to interpret things differently.

When evidence, belief, and desire are at odds with one another, the equanimity of a healthy Fifth Ego Center enables you to think realistically and entertain all available information in order to achieve the best outcome. Equanimity reveals tools in your environment and in yourself to create the reality you want. It allows you to understand that only by acknowledging the difficult parts of reality can you change them.

Ego Wound: Pretense

Pretense is a disavowal of the truth of self—our lie to the world around us. It originates in trauma and it perpetuates trauma, replacing parts of our self and our history with a fantasy that we present to others as real. Because no one knows the real person beneath the pretense, our true skills and assets remain hidden. The world becomes a hostile "other" because the pretender has built a life of lies and being unmasked is an omnipresent threat.

Not all traumatic events traumatize. Seemingly wrenching incidents can be integrated, and we have defenses to use, in the short term, when they cannot. But when reality is so indigestible that your ego cannot survive it intact and denial fails (or needs to be habitually deployed), the result can be a neurological pattern that distorts a healthy ego core and garbles your interaction with the world. Pretense makes us ineffective because we cannot effectively be someone else. We can only be the best version of ourselves.

Ego Strength: Accuracy/Acuity

A healthy Fifth Ego Center knows what is real and what is not. When healthy, it directs expression so that it hits the target and accomplishes the goal accurately. And when others communicate, your acuity allows you to discern the truth, the subtext, and any misleading aspects. Mercury, the messenger of the gods, is the archetype of this Ego Center. He is the voice of the divine, and while accuracy and acuity may not sound divine, they have a magical way of cutting through the noise that deafens human potential. Belief can be inspiring, but only real tools create real results.

Place of Joy: Harmony

Harmony appears when all voices strengthen one another. If there is a dissonance, harmony integrates it. The effortful feeling that sometimes strains communication is replaced by the harmonic wave that carries everything with it without obliterating the strength of the individual voice. Your call is answered. Your message is heard. You participate in those situations where harmony is possible and identify those where resonance is not achievable. The best expression of your being is met with the ideal response. Your capacity for harmony allows you to harness the elements you need in the direction you choose. Everything possible is joined by everyone useful, manifesting a force that can create anything. The flow that results is nothing less than pure joy.

Polarity: Evidence vs. Belief

No matter how optimistic you are, no matter how firm your beliefs, the facts remain the facts, and working with them is the only way to change your situation. When your belief clashes with those facts, that calls for investigation. And when, despite the evidence before you, your reality is detached from the consensus reality, no productive conversation can be had.

But when you integrate evidence and then add the inspiration your belief bestows, you become able to present your truth in a way that elicits support. Sharing your truth using the language of evidence, you find your tribe—and become a compelling leader.

The motto of the Fifth Ego Center polarity is "The obstacles are the path."

Physical Gift: Persuasion

What is your message? Persuasion is the gift that allows you to express yourself in a way that others will subscribe to. Even when applied to your own self-dialogue, persuasion locates the point between otherwise conflicting positions where you can draw effective conclusions, allowing for a clear message *from* you *to* you. When you speak and listen so as to identify what is true, your conversations yield powerful outcomes.

Spiritual Gift: Clairaudience

Your brain is usually preoccupied with what it considers the important information that comes in from your immediate surroundings. It ignores irrelevant thoughts that could interfere with your functioning. But the same mechanism has a side effect: it also filters out your intuition, which is more future- and distance-oriented.

Clairaudience, or "clear hearing," creates a channel for all awareness, all wisdom, all data—past, present, and future—from all perspectives, including the intuitive. It allows you to find the best, most harmonious actions while still addressing the needs of the moment.

Rehabilitation/Healing: Truth

Facts are not mutable. Truth, however, is. It can be changed by time, perspective, new information, and the multiple layers of reality that are ever present. Truth that serves you effectively is functional. Truth that doesn't is dogma.

As you strive to manifest a desired state or result, finding "functional truth" is how you maintain your personal integrity. It acknowledges that what may be true for you may not be true for someone else—and what we sometimes *interpret* as a truth can be "out of phase," not responsive to the moment.

This is often the result of trauma: a truth frozen in time and applied to a situation that no longer exists (or perhaps never did). But "out of phase" reactions require our attention. We need to rewire the neurological loop, using exercises like tapping, hypnosis, therapy, behavior-modification practices, and so on, to help us interpret "the data" accurately.

Injured Development of the Fifth Ego Center

Answer the questions that follow honestly to understand what might have interfered with the healthy use and development of your Fifth Ego Center. At the end of this chapter, you will find an exercise to help heal injured Fifth Ego Centers.

1. Were you born into a family where your voice wasn't heard?

2. Did your family have secrets you had to hide, such as abuse or alcoholism?

3. Did your caretakers have a warped perception of themselves, you, or others?

4. Were you encouraged to lie about who you were or who/ what your family was?

5. Were there significant parts of yourself that were unacceptable to your caretakers or your world?

6. Were your caretakers so overwhelmed that they didn't have time to listen to you or didn't applaud your humor, intellect, and insights?

7. Did you grow up in a culture that valued repression, silence, or stoicism?

8. Did you feel that you had to be someone else in order to be accepted by your peer group?

9. Did your caretakers lack the ability to filter the world for you in a way that allowed you to "hear" it safely?

10. Were you punished for expressing yourself freely and frankly?

11. Did you grow up in a bigoted home where any voices other than those of your caretakers were suspect?

12. Were you lied to by your caretakers or other trusted adults?

13. Did your caretakers lack boundaries?

14. Did your caretakers use words in manipulative, shaming, or other inappropriate ways?

15. Were you traumatized without adequate tools for recovery?

16. Were you idealized or vilified, blocking you from developing an evidence-based sense of self?

Signs of an Afflicted Fifth Ego Center

If you answered yes to any of the previous "Injured Development" questions about your childhood, you may experience the following challenges in your adult life:

You are unnoticed, discounted, mistrusted, or unappreciated by others.

You find it hard to obtain support for your ideas, needs, and feelings.

You vacillate in your beliefs and/or their expression.

You are afraid or unable to express yourself clearly and straightforwardly.

You feel hopeless (instead of informed and inspired) when evidence disproves your beliefs.

You find it hard to be evenhanded, and the world seems not to understand you.

Because you cannot hold to your own truth under pressure, you are often taken advantage of.

You mistrust the world.

You ignore evidence and information in order to bolster your beliefs.

Because you never learned the cues for healthy conversation, you often put your foot in your mouth.

You place your trust in untrustworthy people.

You lie or don't recognize the truth, which makes you unable to be reliable or deal with situations effectively.

You lack dependable teachers and champions, which limits your growth, safety, and success.

The Results of a Misdirected Fifth Ego Center

- problems in the upper respiratory system

- an inability to express feelings effectively

- a lack of purpose or vocation

- constant misunderstandings

- a lack of support for your projects and ideas

- the absence of an acceptable individual identity

- frequent experiences of being overlooked, unheard, or superfluous

- frequent experiences of servitude and victimization

- confusion

- chronic isolation; the lack of a tribe who speaks your language

- being a frequent target of blame

- presenting an unconvincing false front

- frequently missing or misinterpreting important cues that would otherwise keep you safe and successful

How to Heal the Fifth Ego Center

- Tell the "functional truth."

- Embody realistic optimism (a can-do/can-change attitude).

- Deal aggressively with triggers and trauma.

- Listen for the opportunities available from what is, instead of distorting truth with fantasy.

- Be receptive to the help and ideas of others.

- Reject absolutes in thinking and behavior.

- Find empowering but truthful interpretations of events.

- Be reliable in word and deed. Make that a condition of engagement with others.

- Engage in sensitive, honest dialogue with others.

- Bear witness and be witnessed in groups, therapy, or other situations that allow you to integrate conflicting messages yet maintain your integrity and flexibility.

- Respect opposing views.

- Be fair in all things (including to yourself!).

- Practice a supportive voice to use with yourself.

- Teach and find teachers.

- Apologize.

Healing Questions

It is helpful to write down your responses to these questions and update them as you do the work in this book.

1. Am I expressing my truth in a way that attracts support?

2. Am I working to be in harmony with my feelings and goals?

3. Have I engaged in a mutually supportive conversation today?

4. Have I expressed gratitude or appreciation to those I love today?

5. Have I asked for (and been willing to hear) other truths?

6. Am I accepting the truth of the less-than-ideal situations in my life while maintaining the optimism necessary to overcome them?

7. Am I using a supportive voice in my inner dialogues?

8. Am I using neurological rewiring techniques—tapping, hypnosis, therapy, behavior-modification practices, and so on—to address emotional and psychological triggers?

9. Am I being realistic about others?

10. Do I ruminate on events long after it yields no gains?

11. What have I done today to evolve my truth into one that empowers me?

12. Am I presenting myself with integrity?

13. Am I being heard in a way that makes my life work?

14. Am I listening to my own intuition?

When You Heal Your Fifth Ego Center

- What you express will reflect who you are in a way that helps you become who you want to be.

- You will be able to hear both the text and subtext of what people are saying and make solid decisions based on accurate information.

- You will find your tribe. When you choose a path, you will find that you are not walking it alone.

- Conversation and contact will bring joy and opportunity.

- You will have an innate sense of when to *speak* your truth and when to simply *know* your truth, advocating for your best interests without betraying yourself.

- False friends and unrealistic fantasies will be replaced by loyal comrades and achievable goals.

- Your can-do attitude will allow you to enjoy life in all its complexity.

- What you create will be in harmony with who you are and will bring harmony to everything around you.

- When you call for help, that call will be heard and answered, and when you articulate a direction, you will be joined by others.

- Your life will become lyrical and delightful.

Daily Assertions

My own voice finds resonance with others.

I have the right to be heard.

Other people have information and guidance that can help me. I rely on my own inner sense to know whether or not to trust what people say to me.

I have a forgiving and supportive voice of truth.

I am always well guided if I wish to listen.

My truth is a gift to be judiciously shared.

Conflicting truths do not always invalidate each other.

My voice is a gift to others.

When I call, my teachers/opportunities come.

Even when I say the "wrong" thing or say something in the "wrong" way, I'm able to correct it.

An apology doesn't have to be accepted for it to be healing for me.

When I hear my own true voice, it guides me toward my best life.

TWO INTUITIVE TOOLS FOR
THE FIFTH EGO CENTER

Intuitive Tool Number One

1. Write down an issue, a question, or a goal.

2. Allow a stream of words to start flowing through your awareness.

3. Reassure yourself that no matter what information you receive, it will somehow benefit you. The reward for such "non-thinking" is the ability to transform perceptions and create "functional truths" that empower you.

4. Set a timer for anywhere from thirty seconds to three minutes.

5. As the flow starts, begin speaking or writing quickly without pausing or trying to make sense.

6. When you are done, quietly note what it is you focused on and what came up during the flow.

7. You just received information (via clairaudience) from your intuitive, omniscient inner being.

   Remember: only when you accept reality (in this case, the things that trigger you) can you change it.

Intuitive Tool Number Two

Music can also be a tool for eliciting clairaudience.

   Choose and hold one of your coins or write down a question. Then:

1. Set your phone to record.

2. Let a tune you know come into your awareness.

3. Begin to hum the tune.

4. Allow words to come and flow to the tune.

5. Allow this "channeling" to show you ways to bring harmony to your conflict and to illuminate the way forward.

   The more often you hum this tune, the more your intuition will be "cued" to offer you its wisdom and information.

   In fact, you may start to find that during the times of day when you normally sing—in the shower, while driving—you will elicit clairaudience even when you aren't trying!

HEALING TOOL FOR THE
FIFTH EGO CENTER

Short-circuiting reactive states and rewiring them for functionality is a powerful healing tool for the Fifth Ego Center. Earlier in the chapter, I listed a few approaches, such as neurological rewiring techniques, that can help with trauma and reduce the rigidity of expression that we all have when triggered by people and events that bring up old patterns. The more you address these triggers, the more you will be in harmony with what is really happening in your environment and the more clarity you will have to change it.

As you go through this exercise, keep in mind Donald Hebb's "assembly theory" about the workings of the brain: "Neurons that fire together wire together." As Rick Hanson explains in his book *Hardwiring Happiness: The New Brain Science of Contentment, Calm, and Confidence*, "Mental states become neural traits. Day after day, your mind is building your brain.

This is what scientists call experience-dependent neuroplasticity." In short, an emotional state becomes part of the wiring of your brain. How can we work directly with that fact?

To begin, make a list of situations or people that trigger you and when it is these triggers occur. (You should update this list regularly.)

Now pick one, and:

1. Remember the last time you were triggered in this way.

2. Experience and relive it.

3. At the point where you are about to go off into a reaction, take a deep breath. Then exhale slowly while you find a positive "spin" for the incident—a different assumption that is soothing or empowering. As you do, allow yourself to smile and even laugh out loud. A smile, deep breaths, and sending a different explanation to your brain generates neuropeptides that give you a sense of well-being and interrupt the patterned trauma response.

4. Practice this on various triggers.

5. The next time you feel yourself starting to be triggered, access this state with a deep breath that fills your belly followed by a longer exhale. (You may not be able to muster the smile, but if you can, it's a good addition!)

12

Your Sixth Ego Center

Where there is no vision, there is no hope.

—GEORGE WASHINGTON CARVER

CORRESPONDS TO: THE THIRD-EYE CHAKRA

LOCATION: LOWER MIDDLE OF FOREHEAD,
JUST ABOVE THE EYES

The Arbiter of Reality

Birth	Development	Maturity
OBSERVATION	**INTELLECT**	**INTUITION**

Your Sixth Ego Center governs your ability to be in the moment, your capacity for mindfulness, as well as foresight and preparedness. You thrive by acquiring information, processing it to your advantage, and using intuition to expand all possibilities. A highly functioning Sixth Ego Center allows you to direct your actions so they meet with "luck" in every aspect of life. It encourages curiosity, so the world around you holds the possibility to delight and enlighten. In its highest form, it affords your senses the ability to travel infinitely in space and time, enriching each moment and predictively charting a successful path forward.

Properties of the Sixth Ego Center

Life Phase: Birth: You have the right to observe and to be seen realistically.

Life Phase: Development: You are tasked with the development of intellect.

Life Phase: Maturity: You earn the gift of intuition.

Ego Defense: intellectualization

Ego Challenge: objectivity

Ego Wound: hopelessness

Ego Strength: clarity

Place of Joy: vision

Polarity: reality vs. idealism

Physical Gift: good luck

Spiritual Gift: precognition

Rehabilitation/Healing: directed attention

Life Phase: **Birth**

OBSERVATION

Birthright: *You have the right to observe and to be seen realistically.*

Your sixth right as a physical being is to be safe and supported enough to observe and fully experience the moment. Long before objective observation becomes a developmental task, you are born to a set of circumstances that determine how clearly you will see the world and your place in it, how securely you will be seen and acknowledged by self and by others, how powerfully you can envision a future, as well as what distortions will be incorporated into the function of this Ego Center.

For your Sixth Ego Center to be able to mature into its full power, the seeds of most of the following statements needed to be true early in your development (from birth through infancy).

When you were born, your caretakers felt well-oriented in the world. They were able to find the right information to make good decisions.

When circumstances changed, your caretakers were able to recalibrate their thinking, and they felt secure in their ability to prepare for the future.

Although aware of life's ugliness, your caretakers had enough vision not to be defined by it.

Because you were enveloped in the safety of your caretakers, you had the security to observe the world around you without having to engage, monitor, or respond.

Your actions were neither idealized nor vilified by your caretakers, who reflected back to you an objective representation of your behavior.

Your caretakers' minds were friendly places to inhabit. They respected each other's ideas. They extended this respect to your own observations.

You were exposed only to age-appropriate information and shielded from anything overwhelming.

Your caretakers were eager to show you the world. They pointed out and described what was in your environment and encouraged you to observe and explore.

Your caretakers were well oriented in themselves and able to see you realistically while loving you unconditionally.

Your caretakers accurately represented the world around them and appropriately corrected the misinterpretations that may have arisen from your immaturity.

Life Phase: **Development**

INTELLECT

You are tasked with the development of intellect.

As your observations were joined with your increased ability to reason, you were able to engage the world through your intellect. The task of achieving autonomy depends on developing your own perceptions and an expanding knowledge and understanding of an ever-changing world.

For your Sixth Ego Center to be able to mature into its full power, the seeds of most of the following statements needed to be true in your first six or seven years of life.

As you grew, you were able to turn your observations into plans of action, and as you grew older still, your observations helped you identify opportunities and anticipate obstacles.

You had enough adult supervision and engagement to prevent bad planning and support good planning. For instance, if you reached for a colorful pot on a hot stove, your caretakers stopped you and explained why they had done so. If you were hesitant to enter a circle of children in the park, they encouraged you to look ahead to the fun you would have. After a while, your template of life experiences grew rich enough to enable you to make your own judgments.

If a sibling was born after you, you were supported in preparing for their arrival, stepping easily into your new role once they were born.

As you grew, you were protected from situations and ideas that were not age-appropriate and would have overwhelmed or distorted your emerging understanding of the world. When you were exposed to a situation that you were too young to understand, they reframed it in a comprehensive and appropriate way.

Your caretakers and teachers were interested in your thoughts, ideas, and perceptions of the world. Their encouragement fueled your curiosity, intellectual pursuits, and desire to express your ideas.

Your mental dexterity led you to a greater understanding of yourself, and your mind became a comfort and guide in moments of uncertainty.

As you grew increasingly able to understand the ideas of others, your mind proved an efficient sorting station, alerting you to dangerous or undermining concepts, people, and situations.

You had a sense of the right thing to do to reach a goal or avoid a threat, even when, in the moment, there was no evidence to support it.

As you got older, you were introduced to new ideas, which broadened your world beyond the boundaries of your home, community, and culture. Instead of simply adopting these ideas at face value, you processed new information in a way that was uniquely and adaptively yours. You learned to apply new concepts to many different scenarios, enriching your mind with your growing inner resources.

Your mind became a source of pleasure, adventure, security, and reassurance.

As your intellect expanded, you were able to apply it to the challenges of your other Ego Centers. You reformulated your picture of the past and discarded unhelpful or outmoded beliefs that had shaped your thinking and behavior. You developed both a realistic and a forgiving sense of self.

As you matured, you had a deepening trust in your thoughts and perceptions, even when they diverged from those of others.

Your mind was a semipermeable membrane, sorting out useful information from chatter and protecting you from being overwhelmed by things you could not change.

Your Sixth Ego Center defense of intellectualization allowed your mind to manage anxiety by giving palatable explanations to situations that would otherwise have flooded you. Then, when you had gained the stability to do so, you allowed these "explanations" to be challenged, so that you could be more fully in reality.

You occasionally used fantasy—either as a break from reality or to experience new possibilities. You were able to tell the difference between the two.

Life Phase: **Maturity**

INTUITION

You earn the gift of intuition.

As accurate observations were enhanced by intellect, your intuition expanded, allowing you to act, interact, and predict with dexterity while engaged in the pleasures and experiences of life. Intuition helped you create your goals and make decisions that positively impacted your future.

If your Sixth Ego Center has been able to mature into its full power, the seeds of most of the following statements, along with the successful foundation work of the birth and development phases, will be true:

As you matured, intellectualization—enhanced by intuition—expanded your ability to find or create good outcomes based on an awareness of the future.

You were able to unite the feeling and thinking parts of your being. When there was conflict, both intellect and intuition offered solutions.

When your path met obstacles, your intuition found a new route to your goal.

When your thoughts led you into uncomfortable and unprofitable states (regret, anxiety, or blame, for example), you retrieved the information you needed from those feelings and replaced them with actionable ideas.

As you got older, your library of experience grew in a way that made you secure and grounded.

As you reached for knowledge outside your experience, you engaged your intuition to expand your life.

Intuition empowered your foresight, allowing you the flexibility to develop your reality and your beliefs in ways that gave you a joyful path to success.

Intuition made you "lucky," foreseeing obstacles, preparing you for the future, and leading you to opportunities.

The walls you walked into were messages from your intuition that forced you to take a more profitable direction.

Because your vision was inclusive, you could see weakness in others without harsh judgment. You included yourself in that vision.

Your mind was both a safe haven and a magic carpet. In your later years, as you prepare for death, you will have a deep trust—based on a lifetime of experience—that your mind will be a reliable guide and companion during your transition.

As death approaches, curiosity, the gift of the Sixth Ego Center, will overcome any fear of the unknown. Intuition has prepared you for death by providing a safe road back to spirit, and, when it is time, you will transition to a place that is already familiar.

Ego Defense: Intellectualization

In order to defend itself, your Sixth Ego Center may use intellectualization—reason and rationalization—to explain away negative feelings, conflicts, or other disturbing realities. Unfortunately, these intellectualized distortions of difficult situations disable your capacity to address them. As you heal this Ego Center, you'll be able to use your intellect and intuition to find ways of managing emotional flooding instead of cutting yourself off from reality.

Ego Challenge: Objectivity

Reality can be disturbing, and the mind can respond protectively by distorting reality. Negative thinking, for instance, blinds us to possibilities for resolution. Positive thinking ignores threats that may not go away on their own. But *empowered realistic thinking allows us to be objective*. We accept unattractive aspects of reality, knowing we can change them. That same objectivity alerts us to opportunities that life's challenges might otherwise obscure.

Ego Wound: Hopelessness

We are pattern-seeking creatures. We see what we are looking for, often subconsciously. But what we look for is based on our experience. The wounded Sixth Ego Center is alert to threats and disappointments but blind to possibilities. We become hopeless, and in that state even intuition becomes static. The good luck that intuition and intellect strive to introduce fails to be recognized or is reframed in a negative way. Even positive experiences that you know exist appear impossible for you.

Ego Strength: Clarity

Taken together, observation, intellect, and intuition are the formula for clarity, delivering insights that allow us to assess any given situation and position us for success. Clarity may reveal things we don't want to see, but it also illuminates silver linings. It is your magic wand; it can transform anything.

But because it reveals obstacles as well as opportunities, clarity demands courage. It calls for you to become an active participant in creating your reality. When you can evaluate others' authenticity (or lack thereof) and feel secure in your own integrity, even the most challenging task becomes pleasurable. The burden of evaluating what comes toward you or out of you is replaced by the ability to simply flow. Clarity brings luck because it increases your chances of hitting your target. It ensures that your aim is true.

Place of Joy: Vision

The Sixth Ego Center can both see the limitations of the moment and see beyond them to an ideal but obtainable result. Unlike this Ego Center's defense of intellectualization, vision does not deny reality. Rather, it holds many realities in its grasp at once, and from that broad perspective, you can choose the path toward your desired future. With vision, joy becomes available in each moment, because you see that what you want already exists. You can inhabit that vision as you build it.

Polarity: Reality vs. Idealism

We believe what we want to believe, and yet to be functional and whole, we need to face reality—and integrate it into our awareness. The space between reality and fantasy is rife with delusion. But when a problem is viewed realistically, real solutions become available. Your job is to create what you envision from the tools at hand. Effective intuition (the connection to the infinite) must always be grounded in reality or else it cannot be useful in expanding that reality. Managing these polarities—negotiating with physical reality in order to be an effective visionary—is the life work of the Sixth Ego Center.

Physical Gift: Good Luck

The unafflicted abilities of the Sixth Ego Center can create the phenomenon we call "good luck." Your strong observational skills help you make good decisions, spot opportunities, and avoid danger. Your intellect allows you to make good use of your surroundings. Your intuition allows you to work on the future from the present so that you avoid obstacles along the path and arrive prepared. It may seem to others that you are lucky when, in fact, your Sixth Ego Center has simply done its job of leading you to, and preparing you for, success.

Spiritual Gift: Precognition

Precognition is the ability to acquire knowledge in advance of a future situation or event. In its healthy state, the developed Sixth Ego Center prepares you for the future by revealing what you need to know to function effectively and proactively. But if you haven't yet developed your skills of observation and intellect, your intuition will be distorted by the mind's tendency to cherry-pick information, and this can lead to an unrealistic assessment of yourself and the world around you, by making you either too fearful or too grandiose.

Rehabilitation/Healing: Directed Attention

The mind is a tricky thing. It responds not only to your history and experience but also to hormones, neurotransmitters, the normal functioning of your systems (respiratory, digestive, vascular, muscular, etc.), physical obstacles, injury, even light! A good place to start the healing process is by following specific practices to activate the "Fab 4" of hormones/neurotransmitters—dopamine, oxytocin, serotonin, and endorphins. (See the Notes section at the back of the book for links to helpful practices.) Whatever your life conditions may be, to heal the Sixth Ego Center you must master the mind and find remedies for the internal and external factors that trigger reactivity. You cannot transcend these factors; you must address them intentionally, not through detachment but by channeling your attention in adaptive ways. To detach from human experience is to detach from the power you have to create your life. Once you have mastered the mind, the brilliant trifecta of observation, intellect, and intuition restores you to the good luck and ease of the Sixth Ego Center.

Injured Development of the Sixth Ego Center

Answer the questions that follow honestly to understand what might have interfered with the healthy use and development of your Sixth Ego Center. At the end of this chapter, you will find an exercise to help heal injured Sixth Ego Centers.

1. Were you born into a family or a society where you were flooded by information you were too young to understand or metabolize?

2. Were there too many stressors occupying your attention?

3. Did you have to use your intuition and intellect prematurely to stay safe or keep others safe? Did it feel unsafe to be curious and observe without having to be vigilant?

4. Were your perceptions discounted without being considered or explained?

5. Were unreasonable expectations placed on your performance?

6. Were you so overscheduled that you didn't have time to observe, fantasize, or absorb information with leisure?

7. Did early trauma cause you to use your mind obsessively or defensively—or to undervalue it altogether?

8. Did your thoughts make you sad and anxious?

9. Was there no one to explain distressing information and frame it in an age-appropriate way?

10. Did others' harsh judgments about you become an indelible part of your thoughts?

11. Was your childhood so chaotic or permissive that you didn't develop the mental discipline to concentrate on what you needed to undertake or finish tasks?

12. Was reality distorted by your caretakers or your culture?

13. Were you idealized or vilified in your family?

14. Were your caretakers small-minded?

15. Did family or societal prejudice limit what you were allowed to envision for yourself?

16. Were you improperly fed, or did you have physical or neurological challenges that didn't allow your body to support peace of mind?

Signs of an Afflicted Sixth Ego Center

If you answered yes to any of the previous "Injured Development" questions about your childhood, you may experience the following challenges in your adult life:

Your mind is your worst enemy. Whether self-critical or self-justifying, it causes you to miss important information that would alert you to opportunities or danger.

You are very intuitive but not observant enough to find a good place for yourself in life.

You intellectualize as a defense and miss opportunities for growth and joy.

You use your mind as a weapon to keep feelings, people, and experiences away.

You live in your head and not in the world.

You are smart but too mentally disorganized to remember important information.

You blind yourself to intuitions about the future that are unpleasant, leading to disastrous personal and business decisions.

You lack curiosity and find that life is tedious and burdensome.

You live in your head and miss the pleasure of life in the moment.

You disempower yourself by over- or underestimating your abilities or resources.

Although your intuition may allow you to travel to other dimensions, times, and realities, you often miss the opportunities or pitfalls that are right in front of you.

Intuition leads you into good situations, but old habits and reactions create the same old negative outcomes.

The Results of a Misdirected Sixth Ego Center

- OCD
- sleep disorders
- inner noise
- fear of the future
- trust issues
- self-criticism
- inability to make decisions with foresight
- panic attacks
- hopelessness
- fragmentation
- thinking your life instead of living your life
- "bad luck"

How to Heal the Sixth Ego Center

- Deal with reality.
- Test reality.
- Observe.
- Accept the observations of trusted others.
- Work with a psychotherapist.

- Get more information. Ask questions.

- Discuss issues with others who may be able to offer different perspectives.

- Practice positive, realistic visualization.

- Foster a forgiving awareness of the limitations of self and others.

- Use intuition to accept the reality of the moment and find ways to expand that reality.

- Practice mindfulness in a thoughtful, empowered, and constructive way.

- Maintain good mental health hygiene. Stay away from situations, thoughts, behaviors, and people who disorder your life.

- Practice good psychic self-defense. Are your thoughts yours or telepathy? Is your attention with your physical body or somewhere else? The most powerful state to live in is one of mindfulness of yourself, in this point in space-time!

- Bear witness and allow others to bear witness for you. Have interactions where your life and the lives of those you are interacting with are mutually observed and acknowledged.

- Distract from unproductive thoughts with productive actions.

- Make peace of mind a priority.

Healing Questions

It is helpful to write down your responses to these questions and update them as you do the work in this book.

1. Have I gotten more information about one goal, idea, assumption, or project today?

2. Have I focused on empowering thoughts today?

3. Have I transformed unhealthy thoughts and habits into actions that support my functioning?

4. When other people trigger me, have I redirected my thoughts?

5. Have I kept my attention on can-do thinking in the moment?

6. Have I paid attention to my own genuine concerns and taken effective actions to address them?

7. Have I listened with openness and interest to the ideas of others?

8. Have I given myself enough peace of mind to hear my own wise, clear, and intuitive inner voice? Have I addressed physical and psychological issues that might otherwise interfere with my peace of mind?

9. Have I fed all my helpful hormones and neurotransmitters?

10. Have I accepted difficult realities while keeping my sights on the limitless possibilities for change?

11. Have I used my intuition to inform, delight, or heal myself?

12. Have I filtered out unhelpful messages from other people, both past and present?

13. Have I kept my "eyes on the prize" and my attention on the present?

When You Heal Your Sixth Ego Center

- Thanks to good foresight, you are met with "good luck."

- You foresee the outcomes of your decisions and consistently make the correct choices.

- Instead of blinding yourself to what you don't want to see, you allow your curiosity to fuel your joie de vivre, even in times of stress and difficulty.

- Life's challenges become catalysts for learning and growth, and you feel empowered to meet any opportunity or obstacle that comes your way.

- Your intuition is on autopilot—giving you previews of encounters you will have and helping you prepare for them.

- You are able to take in information without being reactive.

- You have an unerring sensor for unhealthy people and situations and instinctively avoid them.

- You frame the injuries of the past with explanations that are useful for creating your future.

- You use your observation, intellect, and intuition to build an inspiring future while experiencing the joy of every moment.

- You enjoy your own mind, thoughts, and intellect.

- You filter useless or harmful information and judgments from self and others.

- You find that your perceptions become a guide for others as you own your amazing mind.

- You have a rich "nonlocal" life. You are able to travel intuitively to other times and places, converse with people, and get your needs met even when you are alone.

Daily Assertions

I know what I want, and my perceptions help me get there.

My vision is enriched by others, but ultimately it is my own vision that guides me.

I rely on my intellect, observation, and intuition to show me the way.

I have an obligation to absorb and deliver thoughts in an empowering way.

I choose what I engage with in every moment. Through those choices, I keep myself happy, strong, and safe.

Other peoples' judgments can be useful information. I use everything to empower my life.

Mistakes are my teachers.

The world is mine to know and be known by.

As I master my perceptions, I master reality.

Doubt is not predictive.

My choices create my future.

I am the judge of the value of new information, and I am a master of adaptation.

Where I see obstacles, I also find tools.

When I deny reality, I empower it to disable me.

Vision is my map and mindfulness is my guide.

I am developing my own unique formula for peace of mind.

INTUITIVE TOOL FOR THE SIXTH EGO CENTER

The more quickly you do an intuitive exercise, the more likely it will circumvent your normal process of intellectual analysis and allow intuition's clarity to shine through. There are many ways to do this. Here is one that works for me.

Select one of your coins. Don't look at it!

1. Take a blank piece of paper. Choose a center point and draw eight lines from the center, as if you were drawing spokes from the center of a wheel.

2. As quickly as you can, write whatever comes to mind when you look at the end of each line.

3. When you are done, look at the space between the lines and write a key word or two about what and/or whom you notice.

4. Now look at the diagram as if it were a puzzle and let your wisdom speak to you. Intuition, especially precognition, requires that you train your mind to find data that often doesn't yet make sense and find the pattern and/or path within that data.

   As you go through this exercise, note the following:

   - How you felt when you were writing it.

   - How you feel now that you are looking at it.

- What changes you might make to organize the information differently.

- What surprises you about what you see.

Take a long, deep breath and follow your third eye from the present to the future. Note what you encounter. Don't take pauses. Don't guide or interpret the information while you're doing this. Simply follow your attention and document where it goes. Speak, write, and/or draw what you're experiencing without stopping to think. Notice if you "meet" anyone or interact with situations. Notice where you are and where you are headed.

Now look at your coin and allow your goal to provide context for the information you received.

Keep these notes and refer to them frequently. The future rarely makes sense in the present.

Repeat this exercise as often as you want with the coins or with whatever goals/questions come to you.

HEALING TOOL FOR THE
SIXTH EGO CENTER

Take a small ball or some other palm-sized object. Note where your attention is and your level of distress. Toss the ball from one hand to the other while continuing to note your level of distress. You will notice that your mind and body become more peaceful as the two parts of your brain connect.

As you do this, ask yourself questions and work with the answers. (You can have amazing conversations with yourself!) For example:

- Notice something in the room. If that item were speaking to you, what would it say?

- What is the downside of a successful outcome to a goal I am working toward? What would I have to sacrifice?

- What problems or challenges do I deny? How could accepting them help me to solve them?

13

Your Seventh Ego Center

"This is why alchemy exists," the boy said. "So that everyone will search for his treasure, find it, and then want to be better than he was in his former life. Lead will play its role until the world has no further need for lead; and then lead will have to turn itself into gold. That's what alchemists do. They show that, when we strive to become better than we are, everything around us becomes better, too."

—PAULO COELHO

CORRESPONDS TO: THE CROWN CHAKRA

LOCATION: CROWN OF THE HEAD

God and Universe

Birth	Development	Maturity
UNITY	ALCHEMY	TRANSCENDENCE

Your Seventh Ego Center governs your ability to access and channel the infinite resources of spirit—the unity at the foundation of all being—to create what you desire in the material world. It allows you to "plug in" to spirit and direct energy to all the other Ego Centers. The Seventh Ego Center grants you safe surrender, the space where you can momentarily lay down the burdens of ego and allow yourself to be reordered by spirit. It's the ease of everything being as it should be, and it brings with it a deep awareness of how to direct energy and attention to expand your possibilities.

The Seventh Ego Center directly relates to your capacity for finding ecstasy in everyday experience and for discovering, when you need a miracle, the place where a miracle can be found. It is the contact point between the physical and spiritual realms. A healthy Seventh Ego Center can transcend even the greatest trauma, providing protection for both ego and spirit while lighting a pathway back to the material world, where you are empowered to make change.

Properties of the Seventh Ego Center

Life Phase: Birth: You are born with the right to belong.

Life Phase: Development: You are tasked with the development of alchemy.

Life Phase: Maturity: You earn the gift of transcendence.

Ego Defense: splitting, somatization

Ego Challenge: fairness/justice

Ego Wound: alienation

Ego Strength: omnipotence

Place of Joy: ecstasy

Polarity: humanness vs. transcendence

Physical Gift: magnificence

Spiritual Gift: blessing

Rehabilitation/Healing: peace

Life Phase: **Birth**

UNITY

Birthright: *You are born with the right to belong.*

Your seventh right as a physical being is your right to unity, belonging—the unique place that connects you to all energy, everything, while providing you with the space (structure, ability) to successfully individuate within it. Long before unity becomes your developmental task, you are born to a set of circumstances that determine how much you'll be able to trust the external world and have access to its bounty, and also what distortions will be expressed by this Ego Center and in the world it creates for you.

For your Seventh Ego Center to be able to mature into its full power, the seeds of most of the following statements needed to be true early in your development (from birth through infancy). If you received your birthright, you had a firm foundation for this Ego Center.

When you were born, your caretakers had a secure relationship and were part of a secure community.

Your family, community, and social group provided inspiration and support for your caretakers' lives and for your own birth.

What surrounded you engaged and delighted you.

When you were born, you were celebrated. From that moment onward, you were so much a part of your family matrix that no one could imagine a time when you did not exist.

As an infant, you experienced safe transit in your physical body—from one set of arms to another, from need to satisfaction, from discomfort to comfort. With every transition came a new sense of belonging.

The energy and connection of those around you seamlessly replaced the oneness with spirit you had experienced before your birth.

Your caretakers presented a welcoming notion of God and/or the universe.

You experienced your environment as safe, pleasurable, and full of abundance.

When you felt estranged from your surroundings, that feeling was quickly remedied in a manner that soothed away any disorientation.

Your caretakers provided everything you needed, even if their resources were limited. They were a source of affirmation and comfort and supplied you with a set of beliefs that were consistent and reasonable.

Your caretakers modeled appropriate adaptations to changing situations. If they smiled at a new caretaker, you knew you could trust that person. If they denied you access to someone or something, you knew to follow their lead.

Life Phase: **Development**

ALCHEMY

You are tasked with the development of alchemy.

As you individuated, you learned to create what you desired from what was available. Your developing ego/self and your still-present connection to spirit connected you with what you needed and wanted in the world around you. Your maturing ego structure brought "kismet" into your reality as you learned to apply the infinite resource of spirit, of energy, to create in the material world.

For your Seventh Ego Center to be able to mature into its full power, the seeds of most of the following statements needed to be true in your first six or seven years of life.

As you matured, you transitioned from being supported by the unity that was yours from birth to creating a world of your own.

Although your caretakers had provided your first model of the universe/God/ultimate power, as you got older, your own sense of belonging and justice became your guide.

Your caretakers gave you faith in the availability of support. They provided a model of how to be generous and successful in community, school, and work.

You learned that everything was yours to partake of in just measure.

Your healthy foundation allowed you to find order in even the most seemingly chaotic situations; your adaptability allowed you to cope without distorting you.

As your autonomy increased, so did your ability to create the life you envisioned for yourself. You were able to challenge limitations in an appropriate way, creating new systems for yourself that brought about positive outcomes.

If another child was born, your world was expanded by being an older sibling.

Change allowed you to discover new parts of yourself and the world, and you were able to create something of greater value.

As you encountered new situations and people, you were able to assess their appropriateness quickly and accurately.

You integrated healthy diversity into your life, and you accepted other people's differences.

Your early experience of inclusion—of unity—allowed you to address your own less desirable qualities with honesty and without shame.

Life Phase: Maturity

TRANSCENDENCE

You earn the gift of transcendence.

Although committed to elevating the material reality of your life, you were also able to find respite in oneness. Your access to the infinite source of energy, love, and connection made you a master of miracles. Even though you were at home in the world of spirit, of pure energy, and were able to transcend physical limitation, you chose to be fully present in the here and now of the material world.

If your Seventh Ego Center has been able to mature into its full power, the seeds of most of the following statements, along with the successful foundation work of the birth and development phases, will be true:

Maturity brought success and pleasure as you easily inhabited the interface (boundary) between your individuated self and spirit.

You had a sophisticated ability to identify which parts of reality were harmonious and which were dissonant, giving you the mastery of an alchemist.

Your ability to accept your mistakes and make amends inspired trust from those around you.

Your energy and your grasp of incoming information enabled you to adapt, change, and thrive.

Your ability to see beyond the immediate and to access power from a variety of sources enabled you to transcend limitations.

As you matured, you became powerful in a community that shared your beliefs.

You were able to transcend reality while still being rooted in it, allowing you access to other dimensions of information and experience.

Your presence elevated everything you were part of.

You became a well-defined individual, fully integrated into life, and when death approaches, you will be prepared to join the energetic plane. Your transition will be one of going from one home to another.

You will die surrounded by community, family, and friends. Who you were and what you added to the world will continue to provide and enlighten beyond your death. Although hesitant to leave an exciting and successful life, you know you will remain a vital part of the people you touched.

As you shift your attention from this life to the next, you will sense the continuity and oneness of all experience. You will be aware of all reality while keeping your focus on the moment.

Ego Defense: Splitting, Somatization

Splitting can arise when crucial incoming information doesn't line up with one's worldview. The ego defends itself by discounting that new information and making issues black-and-white. Splitting isolates the individual from useful people, behaviors, and truths, causing confusion about how to interpret behavior or what actions to take and overwhelming one's ability to find a cohesive moral direction.

A more dramatic response to the ego's inability to process difficult experiences is somatization, which occurs when conflict travels from the spiritual/emotional body to the physical body. With the vulnerable Seventh Ego Center cut off from the healing gifts of spirit, the conflict exhibits itself as illness.

Ego Challenge: Fairness/Justice

Ego is the framework of self, and self is the working, constructive part of spirit. As your Seventh Ego Center develops, you achieve an almost magical ability to make things go your way and marshal support and resources. Sometimes the result is that you wind up with more than your fair share. Desiring more than you can use is a result of injury. However, sometimes you need an overabundance in one area of your life to compensate while another area becomes healthier. You may ask yourself what others who are taking this journey with you need. You have to take care of yourself first, or you will have little to offer others in a healthy way; sometimes enough is not as straightforward as it seems. Assume that when you covet something, even when you have enough, there may be a good reason for it. As your healing gains integrity and wholeness, you may find yourself easily sharing what you once thought you needed!

Ego Wound: Alienation

Alienation is learned. We are not born that way. We are born, in fact, with almost no awareness of being separate from everything around us. But the illusion of separateness is necessary in order to develop an ego, an "I," without which you would have nothing to contribute to the one that is us all.

You are always part of the totality of energy we call "spirit." However, as the injuries of ego development accumulate, along with some of life's challenging circumstances (such as being stranded on a mountaintop), we may develop the sense of being disconnected from the source of what makes us spiritual beings and from the wealth of shared resources that are our birthright. This is the haunting and dysfunctional illusion of alienation. In that state, we lose touch with the reality that the only true healing heals all as one.

Ego Strength: Omnipotence

All power, all knowledge, all being is you. Spirit is omnipotent, and because you are one with spirit, so are you. Yet because you are in human form, you perceive yourself as separate and less powerful.

Our human machinery does not allow full-time access to the experience of unity; otherwise, we would not be able—or motivated—to differentiate, and differentiation is necessary for us to do the human work of evolving spirit.

We can, however, channel omnipotence by the simple awareness that we are both a particle and a wave—one with everything and experiencing our separateness from it. That awareness allows us to find the interface, the position between these two states. Although our ego doesn't allow us to have the full experience of omnipotence without obliterating all that makes us human, the Seventh Ego Center has the ability to channel some of its potential toward creation and connection in the material world.

Place of Joy: Ecstasy

The Seventh Ego Center finds its joy when the experience of being in an individuated physical body meets with the highest octave of energy. That is the contact point at the boundary between the infinity of spirit and the experience of our human senses. Ecstasy can be found in a taste, a feeling, a movement, or any other awareness of physical sensation. It is among the greatest gifts we receive from having a sensory, physical body. Ecstasy does not transcend reality; it elevates it.

Polarity: Humanness vs. Transcendence

The oneness that is spirit/energy cannot create. It has no structure with which to do so. To create, we need to work within the architecture of the physical world. The polarity of the Seventh Ego Center lies in accepting both the limitations of life and its infinite possibilities without escaping into the amorphous ease of spirit.

In a moment of transcendence, your sense organs meet the greatest potential of spirit. Ecstasy is the result. But it is important to remember that you cannot experience ecstasy outside your human structure. When you are healing this Ego Center, you may feel a desire to abandon your personal, human growth in favor of attaining greater union with the source of infinite spirit. This phenomenon is commonly known as the spiritual bypass. But if you take this route, you have entered the dangerous end of the polarity. It is the task of the Seventh Ego Center to achieve a balance.

Physical Gift: Magnificence

The physical gift of the Seventh Ego Center is the magnificence that comes from having access to spirit while being physically embodied. This does not exempt you from your mistakes or from the obstacles that arise in the material world. No matter what circumstance you are in, however, a functioning Seventh Ego Center brings you to the best possible next experience, allowing your magnificent presence to attract what you need and create what you want by accessing who you wish to be.

Every challenge you overcome expands your capacity to experience, reflect, and manifest. Even mired in the muck, you remain magnificent, are perceived by others as magnificent, and inhabit a magnificent reality. Your courage holds the space for others to step into their own magnificence. Your example elevates all.

Spiritual Gift: Blessing

A developed Seventh Ego Center guides you to the blessings in your life and allows you to create blessings for others.

As you develop your mastery of energy, you grow able to change the world around you. Your being becomes a catalyst for good. For example, when you pass someone in need or hear of someone's devastation, you can direct the energy of unity so that alchemy occurs. Your intention to use your mastery for the betterment of all creates a life of blessing for yourself and those around you.

Rehabilitation/Healing: Peace

Finding your peace and creating peace in all situations and for all beings rehabilitates the Seventh Ego Center. This Ego Center heals when it follows its path without merging or sacrificing the self but also without asserting an undue amount of control or power. Peace without self-sacrifice requires that we connect with what is possible in our environment and work in the most constructive way with what we wish to change. When peace is your path, you will find that opposition becomes rare because your commitment evokes what is unifying in yourself and in the situations around you.

Injured Development of the Seventh Ego Center

Answer the questions that follow honestly to understand what might have interfered with the healthy use and development of your Seventh Ego Center. At the end of this chapter, you will find an exercise to help heal injured Seventh Ego Centers.

1. Were you born into a family where the notion of reality was unstable?

2. Were your caretakers inconsistent, depressed, untrustworthy, explosive, or ill-equipped to define the world for you?

3. Did your caretakers have an angry, unrealistic, or isolating worldview?

4. When you fell—physically, emotionally, or metaphorically— were your caretakers able to support you, or were they faulty or absent?

5. Were your caretakers overly punitive?

6. Did you grow up with a sense that the world was your enemy?

7. Did you grow up in a culture or political environment where those in power were a material threat to you?

8. Did you grow up with restrictive thoughts about behavior, diet, religion, or other elements that made the outside world feel scary to you or that isolated you from community?

9. Did you feel that you were the only one you could rely on? Alternatively, did you feel that you weren't good enough to rely on?

10. Did you grow up in a sector of society where you were dis- empowered by your class, race, gender, or other identity markers?

Signs of an Afflicted Seventh Ego Center

If you answered yes to any of the previous "Injured Development" questions about your childhood, you may experience the following challenges in your adult life:

You feel like an island, alone in a sea of inconsistent and irrational energy.

You have no one and nothing to guide you.

You lack the energy and "good fortune" to make anything work for you, and when something does work, it doesn't last long.

You may become a gambler, a cynic, or even a sociopath as you come to believe that there are no rules you can count on and there is no reliable authority you can refer to.

When you see people less smart, attractive, or able than you who are doing well, you can't figure out why you aren't as successful as them.

You are frequently exhausted by the energy it takes to stay alive.

At your core, you don't like or trust yourself.

You have a sense of futility.

Your values alienate you from others.

Your ethics are dangerous to others or to yourself.

The Results of a Misdirected Seventh Ego Center

- hopelessness

- suicidal ideation

- lack of satisfaction with life

- cruelty

- antisocial behavior

- lack of friends, lovers, support, invitations, community, and connection

- a feeling of being disoriented in time and space

- a paucity of resources and opportunity

- rejection or being reviled by others

- unhealthy means of reaching for ecstasy, such as overconsumption, drugs, misuse of power, or excessive spiritual or meditative practice

How to Heal the Seventh Ego Center

- Be accountable.

- Engage in spiritual practices.

- Be of service.

- Pursue activities that induce transcendence, such as dance, meditation, prayer, or playing music.

- Maintain good sleep hygiene.

- Hug and be hugged.

- Visit places that connect you with history or cherished beliefs.

- Root yourself in your values.

- Make hope and blessing a practice.

- Participate in group activities that elevate mood and create unity, such as singing, dinners, projects—any positive experience with family, friends, and community.

- Be grateful.

- Cultivate your ecstasy with the "Fab 4" of hormones/neurotransmitters—oxytocin, dopamine, serotonin, and endorphins. (See the Notes for natural ways to generate them.)

Healing Questions

It is helpful to write down your responses to these questions and update them as you do the work in this book.

1. Have I been of service to my family, friends, and community today?

2. Have I followed the rules of integrity, self-care, community, and friendship today?

3. Are there places where I need to make amends?

4. Are there places where I need to ask that amends be made to me?

5. Have I had a moment of transcendence today? Have I danced, strolled, prayed, meditated, or done something else to connect me to spirit?

6. Am I well-rested?

7. Do I have hopes and dreams?

8. Have I been inclusive?

9. Have I blessed others?

10. Have I worshipped or experienced gratitude today?

11. Do I have habits that allow me to recharge my energy?

12. Have I taken care of my human machine by generating enough oxytocin, dopamine, serotonin, and pleasure-inducing endorphins?

When You Heal Your Seventh Ego Center

- Life has purpose, and purpose holds pleasure.

- You enjoy life and can create whatever you conceive.

- With every change of circumstance, you find yourself in a loving community.

- Guides and teachers, both worldly and "otherworldly," appear to you and show you the way.

- Miracles are part of your everyday experience.

- You know that every failure is necessary for something better.

- You understand that the reality of human fallibility—including your own—is an exciting and forgivable challenge.

- You know and experience every day as full of opportunity.

- Your efforts are acknowledged and admired even when you are in unfortunate situations or going through tough transitions.

- Although you love life, you don't fear death. You have a sense of the infinite nature of your relationships, accomplishments, and sacredness.

- When you die, loved ones see you off, and loved ones greet you as you cross over.

Daily Assertions

I am home.

I experience the present moment.

I create what I intend with the full support of the universe.

All my challenges are blessings, and I am worthy of my blessings.

My life is a work in progress.

There are no mistakes.

Everything conspires toward my healing and happiness.

When I feel alone, it's because I'm not noticing that my brothers and sisters stand with me.

Life is a structure of which I'm an essential part.

I follow the rules, but I also know intuitively when to change them.

My work benefits everyone; everyone's work supports me.

Service is the most powerful form of healing.

I serve, and I allow others to serve me.

I am blessed, and I am a blessing to others.

Out of many, one.

Joy, even ecstasy, is a sign that I am doing things right.

When I connect, I am just. When I am just and connected, I have the power to do anything.

INTUITIVE TOOL FOR THE
SEVENTH EGO CENTER

The demand of the Seventh Ego Center is to know where the pure, powerful energy of spirit needs to go to manifest matter. When you create a physical representation of this energy—an altar—you guide that energy toward a result. Take a moment now to assume that all your physical structures—your home, bed, purse, briefcase, clothing, kitchen table, desk, even the path you take to work—are altars. They are directing the energy we share and creating the reality of your life.

Look at the altars you've already created. Are they patterning the reality you want? Are you manifesting a life of perfection but at the expense of comfort? Your altars demonstrate what you are doing, and they pattern what the world does for you.

How can you change these altars? How can you create new ones? An altar isn't something that simply exists; you must engage with it to activate it. For example, you can set an extra plate or empty a drawer for a partner you have yet to meet. You can walk a more beautiful way to work to pattern the energy of a better job. You can light a candle at night with a prayer beneath it and allow the energy of that burning candle to melt away your obstacles. You can clean up a space to obtain clarity or, alternatively, bring in some happy chaos for creativity.

Do you already have a sacred space to represent your goals and blessings? If so, how often do you visit it? Do you move things around as your circumstances change? As I write this, my husband and I have assembled a dollhouse and together are moving different pieces around as we change and our world changes.

When you see everything as an altar, you interact with both the energy of life and the energy of spirit in a directive way.

HEALING TOOL FOR THE
SEVENTH EGO CENTER

What is your dream? Your wish? The deepest need of your heart? The greatest purpose of your life? What blessing do you most desire?

Right now, no matter what you are doing, embody your hope. Allow the experience that everyone and everything is working with you to manifest your goals. Connect with the essential truth that you are everything and everything is you.

Blessing is the assertion that the best can happen. But don't confuse it with confidence, positive thinking, or reassurance. Even when you don't "believe" or "feel" it's happening, make space for a blessing to happen, and learn to hold that space. You hold true to your blessing because it is what is dearest to you. And you are flexible about the infinite and sometimes-startling ways your blessing can manifest. When obstacles arise, you accept them with gratitude because they guide you to what needs to change and how to make those changes. You make the choice to follow the blessing through every moment, even the difficult ones, to actualize your dream. By experiencing your connection to that dream, you make it real.

You give it substance and a place where it can ultimately manifest.

As you do this for yourself, you will find that you can also become the conduit for manifesting this connection between self and spirit for others. Whether it is as a healer, as a leader, or as a parent, your ability to bestow blessing through self and to others expresses the totality of your connection to spirit amid the mundanity of the everyday.

Right now, no matter what you are doing, embody your hope. Allow the experience that everyone and everything is working with you to manifest your goals. Be part of that same reality for others. Connect with the truth that you are everything and everything is you.

Experience this unity from your perspective. Offer up your fears, obstacles, and regrets to be healed by your connection to the universe's energy. You are guided in your thoughts, actions, and plans. As you experience imperfections, they heal. Your relationships are restructured to fit your unique world. And you are part of this process for every other being.

14

How to Use the Ego Centers in Daily Life

Why do the words that we use to describe important aspects of ourselves have such negative connotations? Ego, for example, which is often associated with excessive self-interest, is actually magic-making machinery for transforming energy. Repression allows you to sublimate feelings and actions that, if left unchecked, would flood and fragment you. Narcissism, in its healthy form, is the ability to see the best in yourself and put yourself first when appropriate. Grief and rage, essential tools for processing difficult thoughts and emotions, have been pathologized to the point where they've practically become taboo. Grief is the ability to acknowledge and sort through a loss and take in what is of value to you. People who can't grieve can't grow. Rage protects the self from invasion. It brings forward our inner warrior. Before judging yourself for feeling something strongly, check to see if the feeling is useful. If it is, acknowledge your courage in utilizing it and allow your ego structure to help you use it adaptively.

Now that you are familiar with the seven aspects of the prism that is your ego, you'll see that there are many ways to engage the Ego Centers in daily life:

As you create change, new habits become patterns, so stay aware of your goals. Your awareness will structure your observations, reactions, and behaviors.

In the course of your day, notice the parts of your body engaged by experiences and interactions. This will help you identify the correct Ego Center tools to navigate them with as well as alert you to new opportunities, old patterns, or dangers associated with the interactions. Here's an example: You're looking for a relationship, but every time you get ready to go out, you feel terrified. This fear has little to do with the Fourth Ego Center (the heart) or the Second (sex/pleasure). It is very much about the First Ego Center (survival/welcome). Use this knowledge to address what might be disempowering your efforts. Do the First Ego Center exercise of grounding, tending to details and rules (dress code, what to bring, what the host hopes for the event, how you can be a useful participant). Do some healing of the First Ego Center before you go out. Tiny shifts in action and perception can make a big difference in how you engage in a social setting.

Shift your focus in interactions by allowing intuition to guide you to the best Ego Center response. For example, if you are arguing, pause. Notice which Ego Centers have your energy and attention, and then take a breath with the intention of creating the best result. Notice where your attention rests. Use the abilities of that Ego Center for the most productive result.

Note what comes easily for you and where you struggle. Use the strength in one Ego Center to support another. For example, if you are creating work products you love but without proper remuneration, focus your healing on your Fourth Ego Center (worth), and you may find that fair compensation comes more easily.

As you prepare for your day, ask yourself which Ego Centers will need attention if you are to meet your goals. If it's a day of pitching yourself, perhaps you need to do some exercises that support your Third (drive) and Fifth (voice) Ego Centers. If you are preparing for a day of pleasure or creativity, it may not be the day to skip breakfast (Second Ego Center: nourishment).

When you awaken, notice where in your body your attention or a physical sensation feels stuck. Do some healing for that Ego Center by either choosing an affirmation, taking an action to support that Ego Center, or simply placing your hand on that Ego Center, taking a breath, and allowing that Ego Center to "tell" you what it needs or what it is processing. Let's say you wake up with lower back pain. Does that speak to a burden you're carrying? A lack of pleasure or nourishment? A lack of creativity? Does the pain make sitting difficult? Could it be telling you to "get off your butt" and work with discipline? Perhaps you need more support for your structure (First Ego Center)—maybe you need a partner or a bank loan. These are clearly individual perceptions that are impossible to address with a one-size-fits-all prescription. But these are the kinds of investigative questions to ask yourself.

Notice where one Ego Center may be doing the work that another Ego Center would do more effectively. For example, is your drive (Third Ego Center) compensating for a lack of safety (First Ego

Center) or nourishment (Second Ego Center)? If so, engage the appropriate Ego Center in the task.

Make it a habit to go through all your Ego Centers and give them a bit of attention every day. Body-scan meditations work for this. I've provided one next.

Make sure to find daily satisfaction in each Ego Center. Balance the polarities. Feed all parts of your ego and your life, even in the smallest way, to keep your life on track. Have you employed discipline in a healing way for your life (First Ego Center)? Have you done something creative (Second Ego Center)? Have you done something that expresses your purpose (Third Ego Center)? Have you cleaned up unhealthy telepathic dialogs (Fourth Ego Center)? Did you sing a song or go to a lecture or concert (Fifth Ego Center)? Did you learn about something new or satisfy a curiosity (Sixth Ego Center)? Did you perform an act of true kindness for yourself or someone else (Seventh Ego Center)?

Notice the Ego Center functions of the people and situations around you. Does your company lack a clear message (Fifth Ego Center)? Is a coworker undermining the unity of a project (Seventh Ego Center)? If so, use the healing parts of that Ego Center to get a positive result. Any physical structure has a prism that evolves in the same order as the human prism. Therefore, a company can use the same solutions as a person, by engaging the individuals in the problematic area in a healing and unifying way or by taking the actions recommended. Sometimes, for example, a company needs to do shame-and-blame pages (Second Ego Center) and then let it go to be able to address a challenge with power. We see this when companies deny or deflect instead of addressing the problematic issues in a balanced manner. Are First Ego Center discipline and rules being poorly communicated? Perhaps the messaging is in the wrong tone for the market and the company needs to listen differently! Institutional problems, even when multifaceted, have the same prismatic needs and solutions as any physical structure.

Scanning the Ego Centers: An Instant Reset

Sit in a comfortable, meditative position. Take a deep breath, but don't close your eyes or relax. Be present, aware, and mindful of your life right now in space-time. Bring to your attention the people and situations that are present and demanding change. As you allow these perceptions to gather, drop your attention from the top of your head to the base of your spine, your tailbone, and back up again, following the breath. Inhale and draw your attention up to the top of your head. Exhale and allow your attention to drop to the base of your spine. Take a moment to experience with each breath the way breath and attention travel together, and, as you do, notice where in your body your breath diffuses less easily. Notice who or what is held in that area. Your attention will be tempted to jump around to different parts of your body, but stay in the spot that first presented itself with that difficulty. Which Ego Center is represented in that area? If you are between two centers, notice where the energy is held most tightly and go to that one. Note the issues and people who arose as you rested your attention in that center. Consider how the healing tools for that center might help you overcome these blocks and the accompanying discomfort. You don't have to recall every item at that center—you can consult the relevant chapter later; the center itself will define for you both the nature of the problem and the most powerful tools for resolving it. Try out, in small, safe ways, the suggestions and assertions the center offers, and notice how the prism shifts the dynamic. It can be helpful to note what the "solutions" would look like, as we tend to forget once the problem is solved. With practice you will be able to perform this process in a matter of seconds; you can do it while sitting comfortably or as you go about your day. You can do it quickly when conflict arises. You can do it as a strong start or end to your day. As you become familiar with the ego centers, your intuition will provide the remedy that will bring about the most effective results. Know that in running through this process, you have already initiated the healing. You can now re-engage in the richness of this moment in your life.

In Times of Difficulty

The following are some suggestions for growth at times when you are experiencing difficult emotions or challenges:

- When you are reactive, notice where in your body the out-of-control, uncomfortable, or destructive feeling is coming from. Ask yourself when you felt that way in your early life. Try to remember how you interpreted that feeling as a child. How did you interpret it as an adult? Use your intellect and intuition to notice if you are now reacting as your mature self or from a place of early injury. Find a more adaptive explanation or framework for that feeling. Sometimes the right explanation has less to do with fact and more to do with how the explanation allows you to function in your life now. This is especially true when it is hard to know if the facts are actually factual! Most of life is interpretive and therefore often subject to misinterpretation.

- When you are facing external roadblocks, be aware of which Ego Centers—which facets of the prism—are projecting that issue into the world. Use the tools for that Ego Center to project in a more functional, goal-oriented way. If you are always manifesting battles, it may be time to look at your Third Ego Center of drive and cooperation.

- After having achieved a goal, use your five senses to experience yourself and your surroundings. What does the world around you look like? How does your body feel? What do you hear, smell, taste? This exercise signals your intuition to lead you toward pathways of achievement that will replicate the feeling.

- Identify the Ego Center that gives you the most strength. Allow the ability of that Ego Center to become a teacher and healer for the others.

- If one Ego Center is doing a job best done by another, rectify the dissonance. Again, you cannot always do this in the moment, but you can set a long-term goal of awareness and adjustment. Simply taking the first step can realign your life.

Human Alchemy

A natural alchemist lives within each of us. You are the creator of all magic and miracles. As you transform your Ego Centers—and your life—you will find that a conscious commitment to your own path heals everything and everyone you encounter.

This path is not without demands. As you allow more power into your life, you challenge outdated beliefs. A life under conscious construction is both challenging and rewarding as you live in the flow of death and rebirth.

Manifestation simply means making something happen. You are manifesting goals and situations all the time without being conscious of doing so. And although the formula for manifestation is simple, the process is rich and complex.

The following is a formula for manifesting your goals and dreams. If you stick to it, you will manifest and create from a conscious desire instead of from unconscious patterns.

The Formula for Manifestation

Though you're asked in the first step to formulate a coherent vision of a life goal, this tool will organically apply itself to every wish and challenge, every question and opportunity that arises in even the most mundane daily activities. That is the wonderful thing about a tool. It becomes a part of you and reforms all parts of your prism.

STEP 1: Choose your goal and state it clearly.

What are your life goals? Can you put them into one integrated statement, so that your energetic viewfinder can locate them? You don't want your precious energy to go in more directions than it must. The more cohesively and coherently you can bring your various goals together under the single umbrella of one all-encompassing goal, the more powerfully you'll be able to act on it and recognize what ego injuries you need to resolve to achieve this overarching life goal.

For example, a "starter" list might look like this:

- I want to make art for a living.

- I want to be in a relationship and to build a family.

- I want to make enough money to live better.

- I want to lose weight.

- I want to heal my relationship with my father.

- I want a supportive group of friends.

While these are meaningful goals, they are wide-ranging, which means they pull your energy in too many directions. Here are some ways to reconfigure and unify them into manifestations that can affirm their realness and don't rely on "I want" or "I wish":

- I am a successful artist, and my art has opened the door to healing and love in my life.

- My beautiful body gives me so much pleasure that it imparts power to all my goals.

- My loving relationships have taught me how to connect with everything that is life-sustaining.

- Good boundaries have allowed me to be enough in all areas of my life and relationships.

STEP 2: An achievable, viable goal works with you, not against you.

Anytime you are struggling with something or someone, that resistance will slow you down. Sometimes this struggle is inevitable. But whenever possible, find the acceleration inherent in the win-win.

Let's look at those first goals previously mentioned to see where you might find resistance:

"I want to make art for a living."

Someone struggling with resistance in achieving this goal may need to confront themselves with the following questions:

- Am I using creativity to avoid dealing with depression?

- Do I want my art to validate my self-worth?

- Do I want to be successful to impress my family?

- Do I want to play by my own rules and avoid the necessary rigors of daily life?

These kinds of issues may require resolution in order for you to find success as an artist. How can you find the worth in what you are doing now or make changes in order to see yourself as worthy? Can you find peace with your family, perhaps by giving to them instead of performing for them? How can you simplify your goal by understanding the hidden agendas and subtexts that obscure clear, direct, right action and then addressing them as separate issues?

"I want to be in a relationship and to build a family."

Someone struggling with resistance in achieving this goal may need to confront themselves with the following questions:

- Am I focused on a specific person who may have ideas different than my own?

- Do I want a relationship or simply a means to have children?

- Am I open to the compromises necessary to a successful relationship?

- What kind of partner am I willing to be for another person?

- Am I using a relationship to avoid important ego challenges involving self-support or self-esteem?

- Do I have an uncompromising view of what a family should be?

- Do I have prejudices that prevent a relationship from developing?

"I want to make enough money to live better."

Someone struggling with resistance in achieving this goal may need to confront themselves with the following questions:

- Have I addressed Fourth Ego Center issues of value?

- Am I conscientiously addressing the challenges of my current financial situation, or am I trying to skirt responsibility or avoid discipline by wishing them away?

- Which ego issues—such as voice (Fifth Ego Center), foresight (Sixth Ego Center), and commitment (First and Third Ego Center)—might be getting in the way of my compensation or keeping me from finding a new source of income?

"I want to lose weight."

Someone struggling with resistance in achieving this goal may need to confront themselves with the following questions:

- Is the number I am seeing on the scale blocking love, self-esteem, or recognition in my life?

- Is my struggle with weight a decoy for my struggle with emotional dysfunction?

- Do I have a narrow sense of what constitutes nourishment?

- Might I be resistant to seeing a shadow side of myself? The shadow is a shameful, deep-seated representation of how I see myself that affects how I present to others.

- Am I losing weight for someone else or for a societal ideal that doesn't resonate with my own values?

"I want to heal my relationship with my father."

Someone struggling with resistance in achieving this goal may need to confront themselves with the following questions:

- Am I seeking an unrealistic response from my father?

- Is my current approach to seeking healing setting me up for further injury?

- Am I trying to heal the relationship from a mature place or from a younger part of myself?

- Am I afraid that the downside of trying to repair the relationship is greater than the upside?

- If I were to change without my father changing, would that healing be enough?

"I want a supportive group of friends."

Someone struggling with resistance in achieving this goal may need to confront themselves with the following questions:

- Do I want my friends to validate me when I should be validating myself?

- Do I create space in my life for reciprocity?

- Are the boundaries I've created to protect myself from the judgments and demands of others impossible to breach?

Negotiate with yourself until you can make a clear, consolidated statement about your goal.

Also know that your life is the map to your goal. When obstacles arise, they are there not to get in your way but to have you clear the path.

When helpful or miraculous synchronicities appear, they, too, will challenge you to integrate these gifts and the opportunities they bring. Integration is an ongoing process. Your goal should evolve as you do. When you utilize everything that happens to you toward your greater goal, everything becomes a blessing.

STEP 3: **Act, don't react.**

When difficult situations arise, it is common to react with old, familiar defenses. But doing so just re-creates an outdated reality. When you were faced with a challenge as a child, you had fewer resources to use. When you didn't get your way, you broke down and regressed. Now, you have more flexibility and power—more, in fact, than you know. When you are under duress, take note of which ego wounds reopen. When you approach conflicts and challenges with an evolved, appropriate mindset, it will change your life for the better.

Each of us has one of four "stress response" styles: anxiety, rage, denial, or depression. This doesn't mean that an "anxiety type" won't experience anger or a "denial type" won't get depressed, but one of them will be your go-to response.

In my book *Welcome to Your Crisis*, I detail each stress response and the appropriate way to counteract them. Here's that information in a nutshell:

Anxiety types create panic and seek reassurance, or else they freeze. They need to find ways to distract themselves, so the anxiety can be tempered and real solutions can emerge.

Rage types explode or blame. They need to discharge that energy, so their natural passion can attract something better.

Denial types cut off feeling and use "selective vision." They need to find opportunities to feel and emote. Then their unparalleled effectiveness will take them to new heights.

Depression types sink into despair and inactivity. They need to use their incredible depth to identify and implement ways they can move toward self-support.

The first iteration of your goal will likely come from an old reality. Instead, direct your vision toward new and more appropriate expressions of yourself and the creation of more satisfying structures in your outer world.

The key is intuition. As you incorporate intuition into your daily Ego Center work, you will be adding new information and discovering a broader palette for what you can be. Allow your goals and your methodology to expand with you. Avoid being rigid. Be open to the parts of your dream that are already blooming. Free yourself from old and repressive dynamics by noticing and managing your reactivity. Get out of your head and allow yourself to become the person who fits your new goal.

STEP 4: **No new damage.**

Old injuries tempt us. The late Candace Pert, the neuroscientist who discovered the opioid receptor, writes about the feedback loop that perpetuates dysfunctional emotional states in her book *Molecules of Emotion*. We habitually seek familiar stimuli, she writes, and retraumatize ourselves in the process.

One of the simplest ways to unlearn this behavior is to ask yourself whether situations or relationships have the potential to cause new damage in your life. Think of the friend who always leaves you feeling insecure or a too-good-to-be-missed opportunity that might disrupt what you've worked hard to build. Think of the third glass of wine that will ruin the next day or the anxiety you awaken feeding on fears, not facts. That is all new damage.

If you must see your toxic friend, invite others along to dilute the friend's presence. As for the disruptive, too-good-to-be-missed opportunity, engage it in a peripheral way that doesn't jeopardize everything else. Order a nonalcoholic beverage. Distract yourself from anxiety and fear with an activity, or create a list of replacement thoughts or mantras to displace the harmful ones.

Take such actions consistently, and you will experience an affirming new thought loop that supports your goals.

STEP 5: Perform maintenance.

Repetition makes habits permanent. To create change in your life, you need repetition with intention. The fruit of this kind of self-tending will seem miraculous.

Be disciplined with your habits. If something is worth doing once, it is usually worth repeating. Frequency is the key. When you repeat an adaptive action or thought, it challenges the old pathology that has kept your life static. Studies have found that it takes a few weeks—and often up to two months or longer—to replace an old habit with a new one. Once a new habit is established, it's important to recognize the cues that signal you are about to regress into the past: situations that make you reactive instead of appropriately engaged or even proactive.

Changing your habits feels like work at first, but when a new, empowering habit has become a part of you, you won't even notice the effort.

STEP 6: Simply do.

Humans are hardwired to avoid change. Our brains view change as a threat. And yet seeking change is what allows us to reach our dreams.

One of my favorite quotes is from a 1998 *Harvard Business Review* article by Nigel Nicholson titled "How Hardwired Is Human Behavior?": "You can take the person out of the Stone Age, evolutionary psychologists contend, but you can't take the Stone Age out of the person." You need to honor the mammal and work with, not against, the fundamental wiring that goes with being human. Your new life will require you to take action, but small actions are often enough—and best. It is crucial to put one foot in front of the other toward a goal. I write most of my books by simply waking up twenty minutes early and writing one thousand words a day. In eighty days, that's eighty thousand words!

If I'm hungry, no amount of reason is going to address the issue the way a simple sandwich will.

STEP 7: Negotiate contracts.

Everything in life is a contract. Some of those contracts were made before you were aware of them or even before you were born. As an embodied being, every time you have contact with another person—or even with an object—there's an exchange. Every time you make a contact, you make a contract. You buy a car and expect it to transport you; maybe it will make you look good or "set you free." In exchange, you support the car and care for it. You get married, but each of you may have a separate understanding of the contract you entered into and, inadvertently, you may let each other down.

Even if you forget that you entered into a contract, the connection remains. Think about a time in your life when a contract got in the way of your success. Maybe it was a toxic relationship or an attachment to a material possession. Understanding the contracts you've made in the past will change your life in revolutionary ways. Relationships that grow over time depend on our ability to renegotiate contracts. It's your duty to find the language at any point in the relationship to address both parties' needs.

Every contract has a formula. These contracts, especially the ones made in vulnerable times like childhood or a crisis, might be exploitative. At their worst, they exchange our compliance for the simple right to survive: Be silent, and I won't hurt you. Support me, and I won't abandon you. Renegotiating these contracts is essential to healing your ego and creating a life of integrity and abundance. Understanding their nature allows you to initiate contracts that are positive, realistic, and mutually beneficial, and these types of contacts allow you to re-create your world.

Each Ego Center has issues. Each issue is reflected in a contract. There are the contracts we are born with, which form the basis of our rights and obligations. I have presented these in the Ego Center chapters. You were born with these rights, and your caretakers were obligated to defend them. If they didn't, they were in breach of the basic contracts of humanity.

Unfortunately, the world doesn't rectify such violations. But knowing that you are born with inalienable rights helps you to reclaim them.

Often there is a superpower to be discovered when, as an adult, you act as your own caretaker—as only an adult can do—and rectify the privations you encountered. For example, my own caretakers didn't provide a peaceful environment, so I was missing the foundation of the Sixth Ego Center. In order to cope, I had to activate my intuition early on. When, as an adult, I was able to develop my intellect and ensure my safety, intuition began to work for me. Instead of simply protecting me from the same destructive situations I had grown up in, it supported me in creating my own fulfilling life.

You can only control your part of a contract. It is disempowering and burdensome to get mired in what was done to you or even what you could have done differently. If a contract was unfair or even abusive, the only thing you can do is use your awareness in the present moment to break that contract—and then be alert every time a similar contract is offered.

Be mindful of the "magical beliefs" in those early childhood contracts, such as, "If you conform to my expectations, you will be accepted and loved." You no longer have to appease everyone in order to not be hurt. And you can reality-test that belief. Notice how, as an adult, you may have attracted situations in which you repeat those old contracts. Instead of getting stuck in them, identify the most exploitative and unfair contracts in your life, and acknowledge the insight and skills you gained from them. Then renegotiate those contracts—and be proud you survived them!

I know this is easier said than done. Like everyone else, I still have some of those pathetic contracts that leave me hoping that someone will fulfill an obligation they never will. We are works in progress! Awareness allows you to work on old contracts without re-creating them in new situations and relationships.

As you become aware of the more difficult contracts in your life, including those you entered into before you could give conscious permission and those you wish you'd done a better job of fulfilling, you may experience rage, shame, and eventually grief. Mourning is an important skill; it is the acknowledgment that something or someone essential was lost. It ultimately paves the way for something more appropriate to fill the space. I think of mourning as the rain that washes away artifacts—sometimes horrible ones, sometimes beloved ones—and clears the ground for what is yet to be. The pain of mourning comes from the effort to stop it.

Sometimes you get stuck in mourning when you aren't sure what your next move will be. During these times, simply attending to the daily tasks of cleaning, feeding, connecting, and so on will keep you occupied until your next steps become clearer.

To learn more about your own contracts, consider the following questions:

- When you were born, what purpose did you serve in your parents' union?

- What was at stake if you didn't serve that purpose?

- Were contracts negotiated (or renegotiated) in a healing way?

- Did you have a specific role in your family?

- Did you ultimately succeed or fail in that role?

- Did you at any point refuse to fulfill your designated role? If so, when, and what was the outcome?

- Have you replicated that contract in your life with others?

- If yes, what would you have to give up in order to renegotiate it?

- Would you like to renegotiate other contracts as well? If so, how?

STEP 8: Success breeds success.

Most people look for signs that they are on the right track. But your entire life is a sign! Don't cherry-pick your signs, and don't overinterpret them. Allow your signs and their organic synchronicity to lead you to success.

As a moment-to-moment practice, ask yourself, "What should I do differently right now to transform this situation, so it supports my goals?" And then make the shift. Remember: a series of small, consistent changes often yields more than a big, dramatic one.

When you achieve success, celebrate it, speak about it, write it down. In so doing, you empower those behaviors that led you to your achievement, and you will build on them—success after success.

Modesty is dangerous. Think instead of the child who says, "I did this!" Now say it out loud: "I did this!" Love and admire yourself and your achievements (and don't forget that there are no perfect ones) the way you wish to be loved and admired by others. You set your own template.

STEP 9: Engage your superpowers.

I'm a worrier. I look for problems and then defend myself against them so the joy and even the plain old experience of life get lost in the battle. I often put myself in harm's way or isolate myself from opportunity to avoid risk. I am working on this!

There is a lot of research on the power of both placebos and nocebos: what a person believes can lead to the creation of either a positive or a negative outcome. In short, what you believe will help you, and what you believe will harm you often does!

Belief, in and of itself, is a powerful tool for change. You can't force belief, but you can find supportive evidence, thoughts, or actions to anchor the useful beliefs in your life. To put it a bit differently: use belief when it serves you, and debunk it when it doesn't.

One of my favorite things about my husband is his ability to find evidence to support his desires without putting himself in harm's way. He has files of articles claiming that lots of wine, caffeine, delicious fat, and sex are the keys to longevity, and for him, it all seems to work. He does exercise and eat his greens, and he takes medication for his high cholesterol, which he insists isn't high—but that's because he takes a pill to lower it! He loves life, laughs heartily, connects deeply. He's excited about his artistry and devotes himself to perfecting it when most people would simply ride the wave of success. He represses what doesn't help him and accentuates what does.

If you are structured as I am, however, it's a task to find joy in the expression of each Ego Center. But I urge you to meet the challenge. Look for it. Find practices that produce it. Make a book of shadows that contain all the people, things, thoughts, and behaviors that take you away from joy.

And remember: *no new damage*. Unless there's a very important reason to engage with whatever causes you unhappiness, just don't!

Happiness is the key to so many things that are good, physically, psychologically, and relationally. As I mentioned earlier, research shows that happy, purposeful, connected people live longer and better lives. Happiness is a contagious state of being. It attracts more joy. Find it. Live it. Avoid what interferes with it, and you will be a joyful person living in an accommodating world.

You Are the Architect

As I worked on this book, I used the tools contained within it many times. I hope never to stop growing, and inherent in that growth are the demands of healing and the unmasking of my imperfections.

In writing this book, I have also found a powerful healing tool for myself. When things are going awry, I simply notice where I'm feeling my pain, go to that Ego Center, and then do something healing to let it—and myself—know that I recognize and am addressing the issue.

Although your individual journey is yours and yours alone, there is nothing more powerful than community—many hearts working together, mirroring spirit at its best. Find communities. From communities. Support communities. Ask for and give help, healing, engagement, and feedback.

Know that moments of hopelessness are not uncommon, nor are they true indicators of reality. Persevere with an openness to intuition. Let new information guide you toward the best way to achieve, participate, and enjoy.

Finally, here's a little-known law I have learned over my lifetime: *You can't cheat. It doesn't work.* If you act in a way that compromises your integrity, you will pay for it elsewhere in your life.

This doesn't mean you need to be a purist; if you must compromise to reach for a bigger goal, that's not necessarily bad. But it does mean that you need to know *why* you are doing something that goes against your beliefs. Take responsibility for those inevitable breaches. Know their purpose, so you don't infringe upon your integrity in useless ways.

In the end, you are the master of your reality. As you consciously evolve your prism in the act of creation, you give us all the gift of your being.

You are always reshaping your ego and therefore your life.
The next obstacle will become the entry point for an even greater goal.
Don't dwell on your faults.

Notice where you find obstacles, and let them be a call to action.
Where is the pain? Which Ego Centers does it challenge?
What do you need to do to catalyze healing?
Now is the time to make the shift. Find the feeling, the
    behavior, the expression of the Ego Center strength and
    cultivate it.
Your dreams will follow.

THE THREE-COIN PROCESS

Before we part, I want to share with you a few of my favorite ways to engage intuition using the three coins.

For most of us, when we're presented with a question or goal, the intellect overrides intuition (and, more fortunately, emotion). That is perfectly in keeping with what years of Socratic schooling have taught us, and it guarantees that most of our actions are based on our information and experience. But, as life frequently demonstrates, history is *not* destiny, so applying an old paradigm to a new situation is often a misstep.

If you want to access clear intuition, you need to trick your mind just long enough to allow intuition to rise to the top.

The three-coin process introduces enough doubt about the question or goal to allow you to "see" the *new* data that your intuitive ability is presenting. That data allows you to respond to new conditions or get a different result from what had been a calcified situation or relationship.

Here is one example of how I use my three coins, which I carry with me always:

1. A situation occurs, and I am unsettled, indecisive, or confused.

2. I pick a coin, and my selection tells me which of my goals share issues with the unsettling situation I'm experiencing.

3. I then allow the connection to be made between the situation and my goal.

This process may seem random, but it is not; it is synchronous. You are one person living one life; it is not surprising that even situations that may seem unconnected are, in fact, connected.

Here's an example:

I was at a dinner one night, and a man at my table pissed me off. I felt like my whole night was going to be ruined, because now my focus was on him. I wanted to give him a piece of my mind, but instead I paused and picked a coin.

The coin I "randomly" selected was #2, my work goal.

In this moment, for me, work is a First Ego Center issue that relates to belonging and safety.

I was able to recognize that this man's actions had made me lose my sense of belonging to the group and that I was responding to that loss with very First Ego Center rage! The realization gave me an opportunity to refocus on a more productive response, which empowered me in this particular situation and allowed for more growth in my process.

After whispering something snarky to my husband (affirming that I belonged), I settled into the evening and ended up having a wonderful conversation with the person next to me, igniting new friendships, and really, in the end, enjoying everyone at the table—even, almost, the offending party!

It also made me aware that I was holding on to a bit of pissed offed-ness around a work issue, and that this feeling was not helping me get the job done and might even be creating some "new damage." I realized that the work situation required a bit of discipline (First Ego Center) to address. I'm so glad that I gained mastery instead of making a mess in both situations!

And I did all this just by reaching into my purse and discreetly picking a coin.

Another approach is to allow the coin to inform you as to what may be the focus of the day ahead.

1. Ask the question (I like to write it down).

2. Pick a coin.

3. Before you look at the number, notice which memories, feelings, people, skills, vulnerabilities, and situations come to your attention. Again, I suggest writing it all down.

4. Note that this new focus may be where your day takes you. When you're on board with what is, you create less frustration and waste less energy.

When I have time and feel like dropping into the center of my life, I work with all three coins as follows:

1. I pick a coin. I do not look at the number.

2. I write everything I notice—inside me, in memory, in my physical environment and experience—wherever my attention wanders. I let all of it tell me a story and I follow that story into the future.

3. I do not look at the number until I have done this with all three coins. And don't mix them up!

4. Then I look at the intuitive responses for each coin/goal. I give myself time to allow intuition to weave together the past, present, and future to inform me of the journey I'm on, what's coming up, and the best position from which to achieve my goals—and, I hope, to enjoy my life!

Again, this process helps you find a path beyond what you already know to the new, accurate, and helpful information that intuition provides.

One final note:

I often ask someone to pick one of my coins and then tell me everywhere their attention goes. I ask them to place what they're seeing in time and to tell me who they notice coming in, leaving, or participating in any way. I ask them to speak without thinking, to allow the story to emerge. I call this "Instant Psychic," and you will be shocked at the accuracy that is achieved when people give themselves over to the process. I taught my husband to be a very accurate intuitive this way. He is a big thinker but was about as intuitive as a brick! Not anymore. The downside is that I don't get away with much!

GLOSSARY

chakra: the energy centers in the body that perceive, metabolize, and transform energy and create an individual's reality.

ego: the unique prismatic structure of the individual.

ego center: a part of the ego's structure that serves a specific function. The location of the seven Ego Centers corresponds to those of the traditional chakras.

ego challenge: a quality of an Ego Center that is both a vulnerability and an area of potential strength that requires consistent attention in order to maintain its health.

ego defense: a trait that is deployed protectively when challenges threaten to disintegrate ego structure.

ego strength: the constructive quality that an Ego Center imparts to your life.

ego wound: the injury sustained if an Ego Center does not develop properly or becomes overwhelmed by life challenges.

functional vulnerability: the part of the Ego Center that is unable to create the life you want in the world.

healing tool: a practice that, if followed consistently, will repair an Ego Center's functioning, whether or not you cognitively understand the injury.

intuition, extrasensory perception, nonlocal perception: your ability to sense any point in time and space from any perspective. The mobility of all five human senses in time and space.

intuitive tool: the non-local or psychic ability that is innate and organic at each Ego Center and can be used by that Ego Center to heal self and create an individual's reality.

life phase: The framework put in place in the first six to seven years of life. When ideally developed, it continues to yield gifts at a higher and higher octave throughout a lifetime. The revision of the framework where it has not ideally developed is the work of *The Prism*.

life phase: birth: the conditions necessary at birth and in infancy for the healthy foundation of an Ego Center.

life phase: development: the conditions necessary for the functional development of the Ego Center's autonomy, from infancy to the age of approximately six or seven.

life phase: maturity: the result, revision, and continued growth that comes from the appropriate development of an Ego Center's first two life phases, exhibited before age seven and continuing throughout life. (Note: All foundational Ego Center development is completed by the age of six or seven.)

physical gift: the material expression of an Ego Center in balance.

place of joy: the place where an Ego Center thrives and recharges.

polarity: the elements that must remain in balance for proper ego functioning and effective manifestation in life.

rehabilitation/healing: the single most effective action for healing and integration at a given Ego Center.

spiritual gift: the place where you as an individual connect with the oneness of energy and can employ it to heal your being and create in the world.

NOTES

INTRODUCTION

5   some of the experiences you'll read about in this book—and that you may have had yourself—may seem miraculous or even supernatural. Scientists can now directly observe how the brain responds to a thought sent from a stranger at a distance or to an image that a computer has not yet randomly generated: The studies attesting to the legitimacy of these abilities are far too numerous to list—and often quite technical. The following papers provide an overview of the field and a good place to start your own research.

Bem, Daryl, Patrizio E. Tressoldi, Thomas Rabeyron, and Michael Duggan. "Feeling the Future: A Meta-Analysis of 90 Experiments on the Anomalous Anticipation of Random Future Events." *F1000Research* 4 (January 29, 2016): 1188. https://doi.org/10.12688/f1000research.7177.2.

Cardeña, Etzel. "The Experimental Evidence for Parapsychological Phenomena: A Review." *American Psychologist* 73, no. 5 (July 2018): 663–77. https://doi.org/10.1037/amp0000236.

McCraty, Rollin, and Mike Atkinson. "Electrophysiology of Intuition: Pre-Stimulus Responses in Group and Individual Participants Using a Roulette Paradigm." *Global Advances in Health and Medicine* 3, no. 2 (March 2014): 16–27. https://doi.org/10.7453/gahmj.2014.014.

Radin, Dean I. "Predicting the Unpredictable: 75 Years of Experimental
    Evidence." *AIP Conference Proceedings* 1408, no. 1 (2011): 204–17.
    https://doi.org/10.1063/1.3663725.
Sherwood, Simon, and C. A. Roe. "A Review of Dream ESP Studies
    Conducted Since the Maimonides Dream ESP Programme." *Journal
    of Consciousness Studies* 10, nos. 6–7 (2003): 85–109.
Wehrstein, K. M., and Robert McLuhan. "Maimonides Dream Telepathy
    Research." *Psi Encyclopedia*. London: The Society for Psychical
    Research. Accessed August 8, 2024. https://psi-encyclopedia.spr.ac
    .uk/articles/maimonides-dream-telepathy-research.

A thoughtfully curated archive of studies over the last few decades in the
areas of research referred to above and throughout this book can be found
at https://www.deanradin.com/recommended-references. It was compiled
by Dean Radin, MS, PhD, considered one of the foremost parapsychological researchers in the world with a long list of accomplishments in
corporate and academic settings. Radin is currently a chief scientist at the
Institute of Noetic Sciences.

2: A LITTLE BIT ABOUT ME

41   **the talented artist and remote viewer Hella Hammid . . . was able to draw
what she saw, and when the people she worked with uncovered a building,
a burial site, an artifact, or, at one point, an entire buried city at a remote
location that neither they nor Hella had ever seen before, it would turn
out to be exactly like what she had drawn:** The following studies and articles cover some of Hella's remote viewing discoveries.

Parmiter, Charles. "Psychics Pinpoint Sunken Wreck in 1,500 Square
    Miles of Ocean." Central Intelligence Agency, originally published
    in *National Enquirer*, November 5, 1998. Accessed August 8, 2024.
    https://www.cia.gov/readingroom/docs/CIA-RDP96-00787R000
    200080019-4.pdf.
Schwartz, Stephan. "The Location and Reconstruction of a Byzantine
    Structure in Marea, Egypt, Including a Comparison of Electronic
    Remote Sensing and Remote Viewing." *Journal of Scientific
    Exploration* 33, no. 3 (September 2019): 451–80. https://doi.org
    /10.31275/2019/1479.

3: SPIRIT

49   the "Maharishi Effect," in which groups of some size engaged in coor-
      dinated sessions of meditation and intention, have changed crime
      rates, raised the stock market, increased reports of life satisfaction, and
      reduced violence and fires in targeted locations: Based on the practice
      of Transcendental Meditation, brought to the US by Maharishi Mahesh
      Yogi in the early 1960s, the Maharishi Effect describes changes that occur
      in the "quality of life" in any location where at least the square root of
      1 percent of the population practices the TM technique. Numerous stud-
      ies have been done testing this claim, focusing primarily on changes in
      crime statistics, with evidence showing statistical improvements. The fol-
      lowing represents two examples of such studies:

      Hatchard, Guy D., Ashley J. Deans, Kenneth L. Cavanaugh, and David W.
          Orme-Johnson. "The Maharishi Effect: A Model for Social
          Improvement. Time Series Analysis of a Phase Transition to Reduced
          Crime in Merseyside Metropolitan Area." *Psychology, Crime & Law* 2,
          no. 3 (July 1996): 165–74. https://doi.org/10.1080/1068316960840
          9775.
      Orme-Johnson, David W., Charles N. Alexander, John L. Davies,
          Howard M. Chandler, and Wallace E. Larimore. "International
          Peace Project in the Middle East: The Effects of the Maharishi
          Technology of the Unified Field." *Journal of Conflict Resolution* 32,
          no. 4 (December 1988): 776–812. https://doi.org/10.1177/00220027
          88032004009.

49   In the well-documented "double-slit experiment," a beam of light is
      aimed at two slits and refracted on the other side as a wave or a particle,
      depending on whether and how the event is being observed: The first ver-
      sion of this groundbreaking experiment—sending a beam of light through
      a double slit and then noting its subsequent pattern on a screen—was
      carried out in 1801 by the British polymath Thomas Young and demon-
      strated that light was a wave, not a particle. Subsequent studies sending
      streams of particles—in this case, electrons—through those slits showed
      that the interference pattern on the screen was different (either a wave *or*
      a particle) depending on whether or not you were measuring which slit
      these electrons were going through. The only explanation that science has
      come up with for this is that *the act of measurement* influences how the
      electron behaves, hence "the observer effect." In short, what you pay atten-
      tion to matters—literally! But how is that possible? There is no causal
      model for this, and so the phenomenon remains a mystery.

Folger, Tim. "Does the Universe Exist If We're Not Looking?" *Discover*, May 31, 2002. https://www.discovermagazine.com/the-sciences/does-the-universe-exist-if-were-not-looking.

Siegel, Ethan. "Observing the Universe Really Does Change the Outcome, and This Experiment Shows How." *Forbes*, May 26, 2020. https://www.forbes.com/sites/startswithabang/2020/05/26/observing-the-universe-really-does-change-the-outcome-and-this-experiment-shows-how/.

Theise, Neil. "The Subatomic Level: Quantum Strangeness." In *Notes on Complexity: A Scientific Theory of Connection, Consciousness, and Being*. New York: Spiegel & Grau, 2023.

49   **"Remote viewing," a technique in which a subject can reportedly observe and accurately describe distant locations they have never seen, was used by the military during the Cold War to gain information on Russian activities:** The term *remote viewing* was coined by physicists Russell Targ and Harold Puthoff while doing work for the Stanford Research Institute (SRI) in the 1970s. Known more recently as "telepathic clairvoyance," the topic first caught the interest of the CIA in 1970 after the publication of the book *Psychic Discoveries Behind the Iron Curtain* by Sheila Ostrander and Lynn Schroeder (Prentice Hall, 1970). In collaboration with Targ, Puthoff, and SRI, the CIA sponsored a series of studies in which "viewers" attempted to describe various military installations in the Soviet Union. Targ reported after one such study that "The accuracy . . . is the sort of thing that I as a physicist would never have believed if I had not seen it myself." Extrasensory perception (ESP), a kindred ability to remote viewing, was also the subject of studies during the Cold War as part of the CIA project code-named MKUltra. Officially, the military has shown little interest in the topic since the 1970s, but various research studies continue.

Srinivasan, M. "Clairvoyant Remote Viewing: The US Sponsored Psychic Spying." *Strategic Analysis* 26, no. 1 (January 2002): 131–39. https://doi.org/10.1080/09700160208450029.

Tressoldi, Patrizio E. "Extraordinary Claims Require Extraordinary Evidence: The Case of Non-Local Perception, a Classical and Bayesian Review of Evidences." *Frontiers in Psychology* 2 (2011). https://doi.org/10.3389/fpsyg.2011.00117.

Zarbo, Michael E. "Remote Viewing: Parapsychological Potential for Intelligence Collection?" Master's thesis, Defense Intelligence College, 1992. Central Intelligence Agency, https://www.cia.gov/readingroom/docs/CIA-RDP96-00789R002600250001-6.pdf.

50 the remarkable data from an ongoing study (begun in 1998) in which the output and pattern of random number generators situated throughout the world were altered (in statistically significant ways) by major global events such as Princess Diana's death and 9/11: The Global Consciousness Project (GPC 1.0) was founded in 1997 by Roger Nelson and a group of volunteer researchers and engineers to test the hypothesis that the emotional energy from major human events could alter the output (in ones and zeros) of random number generators (RNGs), thus suggesting a fundamental interconnectedness between human consciousness and the physical world. Sixty-five such generators were set up in locations from Alaska to Fiji, and five hundred tests were conducted following such powerful events as the terrorist attacks on September 11, 2001, major earthquakes and tsunamis, and large-scale meditations and religious celebrations. Overall results showed statistically significant evidence that something "nonphysical" happens when large groups of people experience a collective emotional response to a single event. GCP 2.0 seeks to extend this research under the sponsorship of HeartMath, which for thirty years has been studying the psychophysiology of stress and emotions and the interactions between the heart and the brain.

Bösch, Holger, Fiona Steinkamp, and Emil Boller. "Examining Psychokinesis: The Interaction of Human Intention with Random Number Generators—a Meta-Analysis." *Psychological Bulletin* 132, no. 4 (2006): 497–523. https://doi.org/10.1037/0033-2909.132.4.497.

Nelson, Roger, and Peter Bancel. "Effects of Mass Consciousness: Changes in Random Data During Global Events." *EXPLORE* 7, no. 6 (November 2011): 373–83. https://doi.org/10.1016/j.explore.2011.08.003.

The websites of the Global Consciousness Project 2.0 (www.gcp2.net) and HeartMath (www.heartmath.com) are also great resources.

4: EGO

66 When you have found your own way to do this exercise, you can see how I do it for myself on YouTube: Laura Day, YouTube channel, https://www.youtube.com/user/LauraDayCircle/videos.

68 new evidence suggests that even choices beyond those simple motor actions are being made before we are aware of them: The following studies and articles elaborate on the neuroscientific research behind decision-making.

Smith, Kerri. "Brain Makes Decisions Before You Even Know It."
Nature, April 11, 2008. https://doi.org/10.1038/news.2008.751.
Soon, Chun Siong, Anna Hanxi He, Stefan Bode, and John-Dylan
Haynes. "Predicting Free Choices for Abstract Intentions."
Proceedings of the National Academy of Sciences 110, no. 15 (March 18,
2013): 6217–22. https://doi.org/10.1073/pnas.1212218110.
Van Praet, Douglas. "Our Brains Make Up Our Minds Before We
Know It." *Psychology Today*, December 21, 2020. https://www
.psychologytoday.com/us/blog/unconscious-branding/202012
/our-brains-make-our-minds-we-know-it.

70   refined by neuropsychologists as "spike-timing-dependent plasticity"
      (STDP): In other words, experiences couple with reactions and become
      hardwired. If your first taste of sugar was paired with a painful experience,
      sweetness will be hardwired as pain. The following articles provide more
      information on spike-timing-dependent plasticity.

Markram, Henry, Wulfram Gerstner, and Per Jesper Sjöström. "A
History of Spike-Timing-Dependent Plasticity." *Frontiers in Synaptic
Neuroscience* 3 (2011). https://doi.org/10.3389/fnsyn.2011.00004.
Markram, Henry, Wulfram Gerstner, and Per Jesper Sjöström.
"Spike-Timing-Dependent Plasticity: A Comprehensive Overview."
Frontiers in Synaptic Neuroscience 4 (2012). https://doi.org/10.3389
/fnsyn.2012.00002.

5: TIME AND HOW TO WORK WITH IT

77   "Distant healing," the idea that your thoughts and prayers can affect the
      health of an afflicted person far away, is another example of nonlocal
      influence that has been credibly documented: "Distant healing," or "dis-
      tance healing," which includes, among other things, such actions as prayer
      (the most common) and the intentional focus on healing from a distance,
      has been studied scientifically for nearly thirty years. Designing studies
      to account for all possible factors is challenging, but as one meta-analysis
      concluded, "The methodologic limitations of several studies make it dif-
      ficult to draw definitive conclusions about the efficacy of distant healing.
      However, given that approximately 57% of trials showed a positive treat-
      ment effect, the evidence thus far merits further study."

Astin, John A., Elaine Harkness, and Edzard Ernst. "The Efficacy of
'Distant Healing.'" *Annals of Internal Medicine* 132, no. 11 (June 6,

2000): 903–10. https://doi.org/10.7326/0003-4819-132-11
-200006060-00009.

Leibovici, Leonard. "Effects of Remote, Retroactive Intercessory Prayer
on Outcomes in Patients with Bloodstream Infection: Randomised
Controlled Trial." *BMJ* 323, no. 7327 (December 22, 2001): 1450–51.
https://doi.org/10.1136/bmj.323.7327.1450.

Masters, Kevin S., and Glen I. Spielmans. "Prayer and Health: Review,
Meta-Analysis, and Research Agenda." *Journal of Behavioral Medicine*
30, no. 4 (May 3, 2007): 329–38. https://doi.org/10.1007/s10865
-007-9106-7.

Schlitz, Marilyn, Harriet W. Hopf, Loren Eskenazi, Cassandra Vieten,
and Dean Radin. "Distant Healing of Surgical Wounds: An
Exploratory Study." *EXPLORE* 8, no. 4 (July 2012): 223–30. https://
doi.org/10.1016/j.explore.2012.04.004.

77   Studies have shown that the majority of our thoughts are also negative
or repetitive, circling around our regrets, hopes, and fears: In 2005, the
National Science Foundation determined that the average person has
between twelve thousand and sixty thousand thoughts a day. Of those,
80 percent are negative and 95 percent are essentially the same as the ones
the person had the day before. A more recent (2020) study by Queen's
University in Ontario, Canada, concluded that we have about six thousand
thoughts a day, but it didn't account for the quality or type of thoughts.
Still others have suggested that our thoughts are not particularly negative
or positive but that we have a "negativity bias." But no matter what kinds
of thoughts we are having, much of our attention during any given day isn't
focused on the present moment.

Bradt, Steve. "Wandering Mind Not a Happy Mind." *Harvard Gazette*,
November 11, 2010. https://news.harvard.edu/gazette/story/2010/11
/wandering-mind-not-a-happy-mind/.

Jerome, Leigh W. "How to Recognize Negative Thought Cycles and
Stop Obsessing." *Psychology Today*, December 23, 2022. https://
www.psychologytoday.com/us/blog/the-stories-we-tell/202212
/how-to-recognize-negative-thought-loops-and-stop-obsessing.

9: YOUR THIRD EGO CENTER

161   The key to healing the Third Ego Center is having the perseverance to
move your purpose forward. It can also, incidentally, help you live longer:
The following studies show the links between purpose and mortality.

Berman, Robby. "Having a Sense of Purpose May Help You Live Longer, Research Shows." *Medical News Today*, November 21, 2022. https://www.medicalnewstoday.com/articles/longevity-having-a-purpose-may-help-you-live-longer-healthier.

Hill, Patrick L., and Nicholas A. Turiano. "Purpose in Life as a Predictor of Mortality Across Adulthood." *Psychological Science* 25, no. 7 (May 8, 2014): 1482–86. https://doi.org/10.1177/0956797614531799.

Shiba, Koichiro, Laura D. Kubzansky, David R. Williams, Tyler J. VanderWeele, and Eric S. Kim. "Purpose in Life and 8-Year Mortality by Gender and Race/Ethnicity Among Older Adults in the U.S." *Preventive Medicine* 164 (November 2022): 107310. https://doi.org/10.1016/j.ypmed.2022.107310.

See also the research of the Greater Good Science Center at the University of California, Berkeley (https://ggsc.berkeley.edu/), to learn more about the effects of happiness, resilience, kindness, and connection on well-being.

12: YOUR SIXTH EGO CENTER

232   **A good place to start the healing process is by following specific practices to activate the "Fab 4" of hormones/neurotransmitters—dopamine, oxytocin, serotonin, and endorphins:** The following resource from Harvard Medical School is a useful overview of how these hormones affect your mind, mood, and body, with further links that explain each of the four hormones.

Watson, Stephanie. "Feel-Good Hormones: How They Affect Your Mind, Mood, and Body." *Harvard Health*, April 18, 2024. https://www.health.harvard.edu/mind-and-mood/feel-good-hormones-how-they-affect-your-mind-mood-and-body.

236   **fragmentation:** This is the division or separation into pieces or fragments. For example, fragmentation of thinking (typically termed "loosening of associations") is a disturbance in which thoughts become disjointed to such an extent that they are no longer unified, complete, or coherent; fragmentation of personality (typically termed "personality disintegration") occurs when an individual no longer presents a unified, predictable set of beliefs, attitudes, traits, and behavioral responses.

14: HOW TO USE THE EGO CENTERS IN DAILY LIFE

281 **Studies have found that it takes a few weeks—and often up to two months or longer—to replace an old habit with a new one:** The following studies and articles show the psychology behind changing habits.

DePaul, Kristi. "What Does It Really Take to Build a New Habit?" *Harvard Business Review*, February 2, 2021. https://hbr.org/2021/02/what-does-it-really-take-to-build-a-new-habit.

Gardner, Benjamin, Phillippa Lally, and Jane Wardle. "Making Health Habitual: The Psychology of 'Habit-Formation' and General Practice." *British Journal of General Practice* 62, no. 605 (December 2012): 664–66. https://doi.org/10.3399/bjgp12x659466.

Lally, Phillippa, Cornelia H. M. van Jaarsveld, Henry W. W. Potts, and Jane Wardle. "How Are Habits Formed: Modelling Habit Formation in the Real World." *European Journal of Social Psychology* 40, no. 6 (July 16, 2009): 998–1009. https://doi.org/10.1002/ejsp.674.

282 **a 1998 *Harvard Business Review* article by Nigel Nicholson:** Nicholson, Nigel. "How Hardwired Is Human Behavior?" *Harvard Business Review*, July–August 1998. https://hbr.org/1998/07/how-hardwired-is-human-behavior.

286 **There is a lot of research on the power of both placebos and nocebos: what a person believes can lead to the creation of either a positive or a negative outcome:** The following studies and articles elaborate on the placebo/nocebo effect.

Brazil, Rachel. "Nocebo: The Placebo Effect's Evil Twin." *Pharmaceutical Journal*, March 15, 2018. https://doi.org/10.1211/pj.2018.20204524.

Colloca, Luana, and Arthur J. Barsky. "Placebo and Nocebo Effects." *New England Journal of Medicine* 382, no. 6 (February 5, 2020): 554–61. https://doi.org/10.1056/nejmra1907805.

Miller, Franklin G., Luana Colloca, and Ted J. Kaptchuk. "The Placebo Effect: Illness and Interpersonal Healing." *Perspectives in Biology and Medicine* 52, no. 4 (September 2009): 518–39. https://doi.org/10.1353/pbm.0.0115.

Walach, Harald, and Wayne B. Jonas. "Placebo Research: The Evidence Base for Harnessing Self-Healing Capacities." *Journal of Alternative and Complementary Medicine* 10, no. 1 (September 1, 2004): 103–12.

ACKNOWLEDGMENTS

When you live between several worlds, as many of us do, nothing becomes real, useful, stable, and reliable until it is confirmed again and again. I am deeply grateful to my readers and students who have lived the work in this book and have painstakingly critiqued it, helping me perfect this system over a decade. Thank you for that, and thank you for the healings and the readings and for sharing your many professional talents with one another in community. Thank you for both the supportive and the ferocious comments that have guided me. Each one of you heals my Prism.

The clarity of my voice in these pages is in good part due to my brilliant publisher/editor/guru, Julie Grau, and her amazing team at Spiegel & Grau, who micromanaged, with great intuition, every aspect of this book. I especially want to single out Julie's co-CEO, Celina Spiegel, Publishing Director Nicole Dewey, Assistant Editor Andrew Tan-Delli Cicchi, and Marketing Director Jess Bonet.

Huge thank-yous, too, to my lawyer, my guide to the world of "right moves" made in "the right way," Eric Zohn; to Craig Nelson, the editor of *Practical Intuition* (and a writing superstar in his own right), who still has my back and remains the most astute of readers; and to Sarah Hall, whose PR mastery has made sure that the world doesn't forget me when I am under a rock working.

A special thank-you to my agent and friend, hostess of the best dinner parties in London, Caroline Michel. Everything you touch is graced by your generosity and elegance.

Finally, this book was written in memory of my brother, Alexander; my sister Sarah; my mother, Vivian; and my friends Rutledge Birmingham Barry III and Marc Slivka, all dead by their own hand. You all remind me that you cannot judge the dawn by the darkness that precedes it. It is worth the wait. I hope not to meet again on the same plane for a very long time and to live every year that you left on the table. I walk with you always.

ABOUT THE AUTHOR

New York Times bestselling author and teacher **Laura Day** has spent four decades using intuition to help individuals and billion-dollar companies alike identify and achieve their goals. She is the author of six previous books (including two *New York Times* bestsellers), among them *Practical Intuition*, *The Circle*, *Welcome to Your Crisis*, and *How to Rule the World from Your Couch*. A sought-after public speaker, Laura has been featured in publications including *Forbes*, *The Guardian*, *New York*, *Newsweek*, *Cosmopolitan*, *Marie Claire*, and *People*, and has appeared on CNN, the BBC, *Good Morning America*, *The View*, and *The Oprah Winfrey Show*, among many others. A strong advocate of using our vulnerabilities to make ourselves extraordinary, Laura gives frequent workshops and live Instagram broadcasts that are followed by thousands, and she spends much of her practice training her students to use their own intuitive abilities to transform their lives. Laura has a grown son, Samson, and lives in New York City with her husband, the screenwriter, producer, and journalist Stephen Schiff.

THE THREE PHASES
OF THE EGO CENTERS

Unity · Alchemy · Transcendence

Observation · Intellect · Intuition

Voice · Conversation · Leadership

Love · Worth · Dignity

Drive · Cooperation · Manifestation

Nourishment · Creativity · Abundance

Survival · Competence · Power